Play Winning Chess

Yasser Seirawan
International Grandmaster,
with Jeremy Silman

D0521427

Microsoft Press

PUBLISHED BY
Microsoft Press
A Division of Microsoft Corporation
One Microsoft Way
Redmond, Washington 98052-6399

Copyright © 1995 by Yasser Seirawan

All rights reserved. No part of the contents of this book may be reproduced or transmitted in any form or by any means without the written permission of the publisher.

Library of Congress Cataloging-in-Publication Data pending.

Printed and bound in the United States of America.

  1 2 3 4 5 6 7 8 9   MLML   0 9 8 7 6 5

Distributed to the book trade in Canada by Macmillan of Canada, a division of Canada Publishing Corporation.

A CIP catalogue record for this book is available from the British Library.

Microsoft Press books are available through booksellers and distributors worldwide. For further information about international editions, contact your local Microsoft Corporation office. Or contact Microsoft Press International directly at fax (206) 936-7329.

The photographs in Chapters Two through Five are from *A Picture History of Chess,* by Fred Wilson, courtesy of Dover Publications, Inc.

Acquisitions Editor: Dean Holmes
Project Supervisor: Sally Brunsman
Technical Editor: Jonathan Berry
Copyediting and Production: Online Press, Inc.

To Min, Lin, and Kit

for all your port.

Contents

Acknowledgments
vii

Introduction
ix

CHAPTER ONE
The Evolution of Chess
1

CHAPTER TWO
The First Principle: Force
39

CHAPTER THREE
The Second Principle: Time
71

CHAPTER FOUR
The Third Principle: Space
87

CHAPTER FIVE
The Fourth Principle: Pawn Structure
115

CHAPTER SIX

Annotated Games

149

CHAPTER SEVEN

The Four Principles and You

169

Photo Album

173

Glossary

183

Answers to Quizzes and Tests

201

Index

215

Acknowledgments

Thanks are due to the many people who made this book possible. Special thanks to Jeremy Silman and his wife, Gwen, for long hours beyond the call of duty. To Jonathan Berry for his frustratingly accurate editing work, and to Larry Sivitz and Yvette Nagel. To my brother Daniel Seirawan, who helped keep the work going in my many absences on the tournament circuit. Finally, to all the folks at Microsoft and Online Press for their support. You were all great. Thanks.

Introduction

As a lifelong lover of books and all things chess, I've often had the good fortune to pick up a book that has made my spirits soar. One such book is a first edition of *Practical Chess Grammar, or An Introduction to the Royal Game of Chess* by W.S. Kenny, which was published in London in 1818.

My motives for writing this book for beginning chess players are exactly the same as those expressed by Kenny in his book:

> Of all pastimes, it has been generally allowed by all who have had least insight into the game, that Chess is the most noble, as well as most fascinating: Kings and warriors have studied it, the former to establish laws, and the latter to plan engagements in the field; the mathematician has diligently examined its positions, to discover the solution of problems; and writers on education have concurred in recommending the cultivation of this pleasing exercise of the mind: at the same time, many are deterred from acquiring a knowledge of the game, owing to a false idea that it requires so mathematical a genius as to be suitable only for a Newton or a Euclid. In order to remove this false impression, the author of the present work offers to the learners of this pleasing amusement an insight into the nature of the game of Chess....

How nice it is to know that the same understandings and misunderstandings existed then as they do now.

The purpose of this book is to invite you, dear reader, into the incredible world of chess. Did you know that most countries consider chess a sport? And that in the Soviet Union, chess is the most popular national pastime? The two largest sports associations in the world are the IOC (International Olympic Committee) and FIFA (*Fédération Internationale de Footbal Association*—here, *footbal* refers to soccer). The third is the FIDE (*Fédération Internationale des Échecs*), the international chess federation.

Chess is played around the globe by millions of enthusiasts. Unlike other sports, chess is constant. Whether on the beaches of Brazil, beneath the Great Wall of China, or at a Texas barbecue, the game is played the same—same movements, same rules. Chess has a language of its own, and since I began playing chess, I've made dozens of friends, communicating with them through the pieces and squares.

Because the necessary equipment is inexpensive, chess has been called the most democratic of games. It crosses many boundaries: race, class, caste, sex, culture, religion, and so on. It is played by people from all walks of life. And it is played by those who can't walk. My first teacher, David Chapman, was a paraplegic. Blind singer and pianist Ray Charles admits that chess is his passion. You don't have to be 7 feet tall, as quick as Carl Lewis, or as strong as Mike Tyson to play chess. All you have to do is think.

When most people learn to play chess, they usually memorize the movements of the pieces and then spend years pummeling away at each other with little rhyme and even less reason. Though I will show you how each piece leaps around, what its favorite foods are, and what it likes to do on holidays, the real purpose of this book is to teach you the four major principles of my Seirawan method: force, time, space, and pawn structure. Each is easy to understand and each is a weapon that will enable you to defeat most anyone you challenge to a game.

After a general introduction to the game of chess, I explain each of the four principles in its own chapter. But you will find much more in these pages. Annotated games illustrate each principle with examples, and entire games allow you to see how the principles fit together. I suggest that you read with a chessboard set up in front of you so that you can play through these examples and turn theory into immediate practice. For those of you who want to measure your progress, pop quizzes allow you to check your understanding of specific concepts, and tests at the end of the chapters give you experience in putting the concepts together. (You'll find answers to the quizzes and the tests at the end of the book.)

I want this book to be fun to read in addition to being instructive. For that reason, I've included highlights of chess history and profiles of some of the interesting—and quirky!— people who have played major roles in the development of the game.

Throughout the book, I offer psychological hints on ways to approach both the game and your opponent. People who play chess are inexorably changed. Their powers of concentration, reasoning, and perception are all heightened. Because planning and purposefulness go hand in hand, people who play chess become more responsible and disciplined.

Let me be the first to congratulate you on buying this book. You obviously want to hone your thinking skills by learning to play chess. This book offers you an introduction to the game that will both entertain you and transform you into a veritable gladiator of the chessboard.

Yasser Seirawan
Seattle, Washington

The Evolution of Chess

We know that chess existed in India at the beginning of the 7th century, and we have evidence that a form of chess existed in central Asia in the 1st century. Some people claim that the game might date back as far as the 15th century B.C. Nobody knows exactly how old chess is.

From India, chess quickly spread to Persia and thence to Arabia, where powerful rulers patronized good players in the same manner that European nobility would later patronize musicians and artists. Chess first came to Europe when the Moors conquered Spain in the 8th century. Within a century or two, chess was being played throughout Europe, including Russia, spread by either soldiers or traders.

Whereas the countries of East Asia adapted the rules of the game and the board to local customs, Europe adopted the Muslim form of chess and played it for six centuries without change. Then the game changed dramatically, turning chess from a stodgy game of slow advances into a game of lightning strikes and constant action. You'll learn more about this change when we talk about the way the Queen moves.

In Europe, chess was played mostly by people in religious orders and royal courts. Not until the 19th century were clubs founded and tournaments organized, thereby giving chess a wider following. Soon thereafter, a World Champion was crowned, and professional chess players began to appear for the first time. Chess literature began to proliferate as ordinary people came to love the game. Today, chess is played in virtually every country in the world. With tens of thousands of competitions and hundreds of magazines, chess is the world's most popular board game and one of the most beloved of all games.

Why Play Chess?

You would be foolish indeed if you played chess simply to win. You can always find opponents who are weaker than you are to ensure that you win game after game. But what would be the point? You would become bored, your game wouldn't improve, and you'd miss out on the fun of constantly learning more about chess. You should always seek out opponents equal or superior to yourself. You will certainly lose your share of games, but your victories will be sweeter and the lessons from the losses will strengthen your play.

I play chess because it enables me to engage in a physically safe but psychologically strenuous battle in which I pit my wits against those of my opponent. Complex strategies that include vicious attacks and subtle defenses take me beyond the thrill of competition and into the realms of the creative process, of art. Each game demands an ordered mind and deep concentration, and can result not only in a deeply satisfying victory on the chessboard, but also in an improvement in my daily life due to the mental focus that playing chess develops in me.

This anonymous chess saying nicely sums up the reasons why most of us play chess:

Chess, like love, like music, has the power to make men happy.

Young or old, black or white, male or female, jock or couch potato, cook or computer programmer—everyone can learn how to play chess and know the satisfaction of unleashing their creative and combative potential at the chessboard. Chess is in many ways a great equalizer. Having said that, I have to acknowledge that, perplexingly, chess is a great bastion of male chauvinism.

Women in Chess

Unlike other sports where physical prowess determines the outcome, you would think that chess would allow men and women to compete on an equal level. Shockingly, males dominate the sport of chess. There are no women among the world's top 100 players. The Women's World Champion, Maya Chiburdanidze, has a numerical rating of 2500, compared with a rating of 2800 for Garry Kasparov, the World Champion. Professional chess players consider a Grandmaster to be a "class" better than a Grandmaster with 50 fewer rating points. What makes Kasparov six "classes" better than Chiburdanidze? I don't know. I can only say that so complete is male domination of the chess world that very few women have earned the Grandmaster title. In an insult to women everywhere, FIDE simply lowered the performance level required for women to earn titles, thereby adding a new twist to the mysterious world of chess. (FIDE is an acronym for *Fédération Internationale des Échecs*, the international chess federation.) Women can now earn Woman Grandmaster (WGM) and Woman International Master (WIM) titles.

Bowing to tradition, in this book I refer to all chess players as *he*. To those readers who might find the exclusive use of this pronoun offensive, I apologize. It reflects the current reality of the chess world. I encourage female chess players everywhere to change that reality.

Necessary Equipment

The Chessboard

The chessboard is a square, checkered board of 64 alternately colored squares, 8 from top to bottom and 8 from side to side. The squares can be any size.

The board can be made of virtually any material. The more expensive, wooden boards are suitable for use at home, whereas the folding vinyl or plastic boards are perfect for carrying around. If no other board is available, you can easily make one from cloth. Failing that, you can always draw one on the floor, though other members of your household may not approve of this solution.

Putting Color into the Game

Throughout the history of chess, the 8 x 8 board has been the standard in almost every country. However, the squares were not differentiated by color in the early years of the game. A European innovation in the 11th century added dark and light shades and led to the dark and light squares of modern boards.

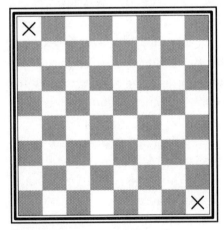

DIAGRAM 1.

The best colors for chessboards are brown or green and off-white. Black and red boards are too glaring on the eyes and are never used in competitions.

Before setting up your pieces, always make sure that the square in the bottom right corner is light colored (see Diagram 1). The rule for chess players and dieters is: Light is right.

The Chessmen

At the start of a game, each player has an army of 16 men, consisting of eight pieces and eight pawns. The pieces include a King, a Queen, two Bishops, two Knights, and two Rooks. The goal of the game is to capture your opponent's King, so the King is in a class of its own. The other pieces are divided into two groups: the Bishops and Knights are minor pieces, and the Rooks and the Queen are major pieces.

The two armies are distinguished by their color. For obvious reasons, the player with the lighter-colored army is referred to as *White*, and the player with the darker-colored army is referred to as *Black*. By tradition, when discussing particular games, the name of the person playing White is always given first. For example, in the Karl Anderssen–Ignác Kolisch match mentioned in the next section, Anderssen is White and Kolisch is Black.

Today, most chess sets are variations of a classic design by Englishman Howard Staunton (1810–74). Later in this chapter, you will see photographs of Staunton chessmen.

Chess Timers

The scene: a tournament in the mid 1800s. Paul Morphy (considered by many people to be the greatest player of all time) is becoming agitated. His opponent, Louis Paulsen, has been deliberating over his move for 9 hours. Morphy, usually the epitome of politeness and certainly one of the quickest players around, finally feels the need to ask, "Excuse me, why aren't you making a move?" Paulsen comes to life with a jerk: "Oh, I thought it was your move!"

Incidents such as this one prompted the idea that games should be timed, and in 1861 the Karl Anderssen–Ignác Kolisch match in London introduced the concept of timed games to the world by timing the match with an hourglass for each player.

Technology soon left the hourglass behind. When Wilhelm Steinitz established himself as the world's best player by defeating Anderssen in 1866, the games were timed by independent clocks. By the 1880s, the first mechanical, double chess clock had been invented.

Today, on the international scene, each player commonly has 2 hours to complete 40 moves. Other time limits are also used, though, with Blitz chess (where each player has 5 minutes for the entire game!) being particularly exciting and popular.

A chess clock consists of two timers attached to each other or set side by side. Whereas a chessboard is mandatory equipment, a chess clock is necessary only for tournaments. You can enjoy chess for a lifetime and never use a clock.

The idea behind using a chess clock is to allow each player only a certain amount of thinking time. Let's say that you are playing a game in which each side is allowed 1 hour for the whole game. While you are thinking over your move, your timer ticks away the precious minutes of your hour. When you make a move, you reach over to the clock and press the button closest to you. Your timer stops and the timer of your opponent starts. Your opponent does likewise. To win the game, you must either checkmate your opponent, force him to give up, or present him with such difficult problems that he uses up all his time and, as a result, forfeits the game.

Today, two types of clocks are used. Most common is the old mechanical, windup style. These clocks usually range in price from about $50 to $80. A popular alternative is the digital clock, preferred by many people because it displays the remaining time to the second. Digital clocks tend to be more expensive than mechanical clocks—ranging anywhere from $60 to $120.

If you don't own a clock but want to time your games, you can use a tape recorder to sound a beep every 10 seconds. When you hear the beep, you must make your move or suffer some dire consequence—forfeiture of the game is the usual penalty, but you can be creative: loss of all your worldly possessions, exile to a remote island where nobody plays chess, and so forth.

Reading and Writing Chess Moves

Before I can describe how to set up the chessboard and how to move the pieces and pawns, I need to explain algebraic chess notation. Many ways of writing down chess moves have been tried over the years, but algebraic notation has become increasingly popular in the last couple of centuries. Today, it is the only notation recognized by FIDE.

Besides its ease of use, algebraic notation is particularly valuable because it is essentially the same in all languages. The only difference from language to language is the letter used to denote the piece being moved. For example, in English a Bishop is represented by a B. In German a Bishop is called a *Laufer* (which actually means *runner*), so an L represents this piece. However, if the Bishop is being moved to square c4, the move is written similarly: Bc4 or Lc4.

No matter which notation is used, the following symbols always mean the same thing: !—excellent move; !!—brilliant move; ?—poor move; ??—gross blunder; ?!—dubious move; and !?—interesting move.

Mastering Algebraic Notation

At one time or another, everyone has glanced through a chess book or at the chess column in a newspaper and noticed strange combinations of letters and numbers that obviously constitute a secret code decipherable only by genius cryptographers.

Not so. Algebraic chess notation is easy to learn. But don't tell anybody. Let your friends be amazed by your brilliance, and let your family think that you have just mastered an ancient language. This illusion

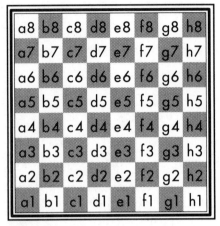

DIAGRAM 2.

might be useful if you take a trip: "I have to stop over in Washington, dear. The Smithsonian wants me to look at a new codex they just dug up."

Diagram 2 tells just about all you need to know as far as algebraic notation is concerned. By convention, chess diagrams always show White playing from the bottom and Black playing from the top.

The eight files (rows that run left to right for White and right to left for Black) are indicated by the small letters a, b, c, d, e, f, g, and h, respectively. The eight ranks (columns that run from bottom to top for White and from top to bottom for Black) are numbered 1 through 8. In the starting position, the White pieces and pawns are placed on the 1st and 2nd ranks, and the Black pieces and pawns are placed on the 7th and 8th ranks. (I'll cover how to set up the pieces and pawns and how to move

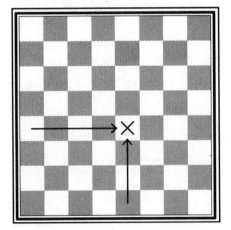

DIAGRAM 3.

them later in this chapter.)

As you can see in Diagram 2, this letter/number scheme gives each individual square a permanent "name." Don't bother memorizing these names. Instead, simply join together the file letter and the rank number.

Let's look at Diagram 3 as an illustration. If a piece is moved to the X'ed square, you simply combine the file's letter and the rank's number to obtain the square's name—in this case, e4. Then place the first letter of the piece being moved in front of the square's name. For example, if you move your King to the X'ed square, you write Ke4. If you move your Bishop to that square, you write Be4. To avoid confusion with the King, a Knight is indicated by N, so if you move your Knight to that square, you write Ne4. A Rook would be Re4, and a Queen would be Qe4. Pawn moves are recognized by the absence of any letter. Thus, if you move a pawn to e4, simply write e4.

Captures are indicated by an x. If a Knight captures another piece on e4, you write the move as Nxe4. When a pawn makes a capture, you must also record the file from which it came. Thus, moving a pawn from f3 to capture something on e4 is written like this: fxe4.

Here is another rule concerning algebraic notation:

■ If two identical pieces can go to the same square, you must clearly identify which piece is being moved.

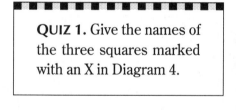

QUIZ 1. Give the names of the three squares marked with an X in Diagram 4.

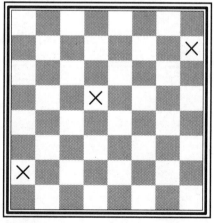

DIAGRAM 4.

For example, Diagram 5 shows White Knights on both c3 and g3. If one of the Knights moves to square e4, you cannot write Ne4 because that notation doesn't indicate which Knight moved. Writing Nce4 makes it clear that the c3-Knight moved.

Diagram 6 shows another problem that you might run into. Here, both Knights are on the c-file and they can both move to e4. Writing Nce4 would not help at all here. Instead, N3e4 shows that the Knight on the 3rd rank is the one that is going to e4.

The next four notation rules may not make much sense to you if you are completely new to chess. Don't panic! I'll cover the four moves in question in detail later in the book. Their notation rules are included here so that you'll have all the rules in one place for future reference.

- Castling involves moving the King and the Rook at the same time. You use one of two castling notations, depending on which Rook is involved in the move. If the Rook on either h1 or h8 is involved, the move is written O-O. If the Rook on either a1 or a8 is involved, the move is written O-O-O. Castling is explained on page 29.

DIAGRAM 5.

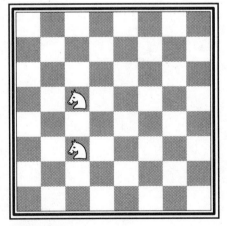

DIAGRAM 6.

- An en passant capture is shown by placing *e.p.* after the move. I discuss the en passant rule on page 27.

- If you check your opponent's King, you write either *ch* or + after the move. In this book, I will use +. Check and checkmate are discussed on page 22.

- If you promote a pawn to a piece, you simply write the move made by the pawn and say which piece it turns into. For example, in Diagram 7, if you move the pawn on e7 to e8 and promote it to a Queen, you write e8=Q; if you promote it to a Knight, you write e8=N. I discuss pawn promotion on page 21.

I should mention one other notation convention. A complete move consists of a move number followed by White's move and then Black's move, like this: 1.e4 e5. In game annotations (commentary), it is often necessary to discuss first White's move and then Black's move. White's move presents no problems: 1.e4 is obviously White's move. To avoid confusion when discussing Black's move, the convention is to replace White's move with three periods, as in 1...e5.

That's all there is to algebraic notation! Don't let it scare you. With a little practice, it will become second nature.

DIAGRAM 7.

How to Set Up the Board

Chessmen have been placed in the same starting positions for centuries. Some players, afraid that chess is becoming played out, have recommended different starting setups. Though these other arrangements are interesting, they have never really caught on. There is still only one accepted way to set up the chessboard.

DIAGRAM 8.

Diagram 8 shows all the pieces and pawns in their starting positions. Note the King and Queen in the middle, the Bishops on either side of them, and further out, the Knights and the Rooks. The pawns are lined up in front of the pieces, like foot soldiers on parade.

The main point of confusion for some people is where to place the King and Queen. Does the King go on the right or the left? Here's a simple rule to help you remember:

Always put the Queen on her color.

In the diagram you can see that the White Queen is on a light square and the Black Queen is on a dark square.

Dividing the Board

The chessboard is divided into areas known as the *Kingside* and the *Queenside*. White's Kingside is all the squares in the e1-e4-h4-h1 rectangle, and his Queenside is all the squares in the d1-d4-a4-a1 rectangle. Black's Kingside is all the squares in the e8-e5-h5-h8 rectangle, and his Queenside is all the squares in the d8-d5-a5-a8 rectangle.

■■■■■■■■■■■■■■■■■■■■■■■■■■■■■■■■■■■■

QUIZ 2. Take all the men off your board, put this book down, and then set up the pieces and pawns in their correct positions.

How to Move the Pieces and Pawns

At last, you are ready to learn how to move the pieces! You will be surprised at just how easy it is. When I was in junior high school, a friend of mine learned how to play chess. His mother paid him a classic backhanded compliment, "That's very good, dear, but it takes years to learn how to play real chess." Most people share this misconception about the difficulty of chess. Although it is true that chess is a hard game to master, you'll have no problem at all learning the rules and enjoying the game right away.

In chess, the two players move in turn. You can't skip a move or pass, even if making a move means you will lose the game. And while we're dealing with the basics, I might as well introduce one quick fact that concerns all the pieces: Besides the Knight, no piece can change directions mid-move! You cannot start moving your piece in one direction and then, during the same move, change directions, zigzagging all over the board like some berserk mouse in a maze. Only when you start your next move can you change the direction in which a piece is traveling.

As you move about the board, you need to be alert to opportunities to capture your opponent's pieces and pawns. Capturing an enemy piece or pawn is a simple matter of moving your piece or pawn to the square occupied by the enemy piece and lifting it off the board. Other than the King, any piece can be captured. (For the King, inevitable capture ends the game before the actual capture is carried out.)

The pieces and pawns are known collectively as *material*. If you capture one of your opponent's pieces, you have gained material. If he then captures your equivalent piece, he is said to have recaptured that piece and material is said to be even.

The King's Stately Pace

The King has always represented a monarch, from a Rajah in India, to a Shah in Persia, to a Roi in France. The King is the most important piece on the board simply because its capture represents the loss of the game. The fact that the King is the most important piece by no means makes it the most powerful. It can't jump over other pieces (as the Knight can), and it can't sacrifice itself.

The King has always moved exactly as it does today, except that castling, a King–Rook maneuver described on page 29, was not invented until about the 13th century. The King can move one square in any direction, be it horizontally, vertically, or diagonally, and it can move both forward and backward. Diagram 9 shows the King's sphere of influence from square c5.

The Birth of a Queen

More than 1400 years ago, in the original Indian game of Chaturanga, the Queen was the weakest piece, its moves being limited to the four squares diagonally adjacent to the square the Queen was sitting on. At that time, the piece was not known as the Queen, but rather as the Mantri, which in English means *adviser to the King*. When the game spread to Persia, the Mantri became the Firzan (which means *wise man*). In Europe, the name was never translated literally. From the early days, the piece was

14

known as the Lady (the Dama in Spanish). Because Europeans thought it natural for the King to have a consort, in many countries the Lady became the Queen.

Around 1475, the Queen's moves were extended to make it the most powerful piece on the board. The Italians characterized the new piece as *furioso* and the new game as *scacchi alla rabioso* (rabid chess), which has nothing to do with the mental state of chess players!

With the combined powers of a Bishop and a Rook, the Queen has the ability to control an amazing number of squares. In any one move, the Queen can move any distance horizontally, vertically, or diagonally. It can move backward but cannot jump over other pieces. Diagram 10 shows the Queen's sphere of influence from square c5.

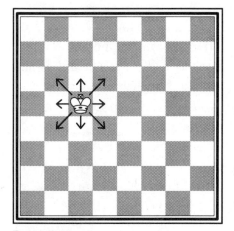

DIAGRAM 9.

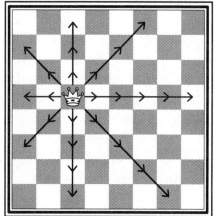

DIAGRAM 10.

The Rook Is Not a Castle

Until the 15th century when the Queen became the most powerful piece, the Rook reigned supreme. So important was this piece that a player attacking it was expected to show his manners by saying "Check-rook."

Though the Rook's powers have not changed throughout the history of chess, its name has undergone various transformations. Originally called a Ratha (Sanskrit for *chariot*), it traveled to Europe under the Arabic name Rukh. The Italians used the like-sounding name Rocco (which means *tower*). Because the Rook is a small tower, Western Europeans followed the lead of the Italians in two ways: They either used the word for *tower* from their own language (Tour in French), or they used a word that sounded like Rocco (Rook in English). Thus, though a chariot vaguely resembles a tower on wheels, it was more the chance similarity between the sound of an Arabic and an Italian word and the connection between towers and kings that gave us the modern Rook.

Some players incorrectly call the Rook a Castle. If you hear the name Castle, don't bother pointing out the mistake, however. Calling the Rook a Castle is about the smallest error you can make in chess, because everybody understands which piece you mean.

The Rook is one of the strongest chess pieces. It can move one or more squares on any file or rank. Like most other pieces, the Rook cannot jump over enemy or friendly pieces, but it can move backward, forward, and sideways. It can move only horizontally or vertically, not diagonally.

In old Indian chess sets, the Rook has the shape of a chariot—an appropriate analogy for a piece that blasts down open files and ranks with great speed and force. Diagram 11 shows the Rook's sphere of influence from square c5.

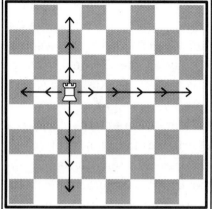

DIAGRAM 11.

DIAGRAM 12.

QUIZ 3. Can the White Rook capture anything from the position shown in Diagram 12? What is White's best move?

Elephant, Runner, and Finally Bishop

The predecessor of the modern Bishop was the Fil or Al-fil (meaning *elephant*). It was a much weaker piece than its modern counterpart because it could only leap diagonally across one square.

Europeans, who had never seen an elephant, had a tough time fitting this animal into the royal court. As time went on, this piece was called the Alfiere (meaning *standard-bearer*) by the Italians and the Laufer (meaning *runner*) by the Germans. In France, the stylized elephant of the Indian chess set was thought to look like a court jester's cap, so the piece became known as the Fou (meaning *fool*). In England, the piece was thought to resemble a bishop's mitre, a symbol that fit well with the power structure of the day: King, Queen, and Church.

The Bishop is considered to be about equal in value to a Knight, though many chess writers give the Bishop a small edge. By the end of the 15th century, the Bishop had lost its power to leap across a square but had gained long-range maneuverability on the diagonal, with the ability to move backward or forward. Like the Rook, King, and Queen, the Bishop cannot jump over other pieces.

The Bishop's one weakness is that it is limited to squares of one color throughout the game. This restriction hurts the effectiveness of a single Bishop, but two Bishops working together can cut through an opponent's position like a pair of scissors. As a team, they are powerful indeed.

Diagram 13 shows the Bishop's sphere of influence from square c5.

QUIZ 4. In Diagram 14, could one Bishop ever capture the other?

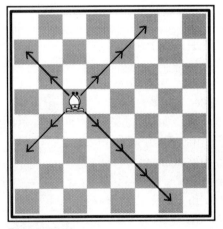

DIAGRAM 13.

DIAGRAM 14.

The Noble Knight

Unchanged in 1400 years, the Knight has had variations of the same shape and has moved around the board in the same way since the invention of the game. It was known as a horse to the Indians, Persians, and Arabs, and because the horse was readily identifiable to Europeans, in many countries the name remained the same. In other countries, including England and France, the horse acquired a rider and became a Knight, bringing this piece in line with the ethic of chivalry associated with the King, Queen, and Bishop.

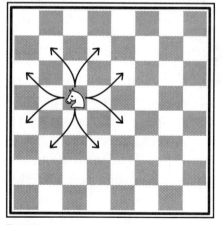

Most beginning chess players have a love-hate relationship with the Knight. They love the weird way the Knight moves, leaping on unsuspecting opponent's pieces. But they fear the enemy Knight's ability to hop all over the place and wipe out their own pieces. With experience, many players—myself included—develop a special fondness for the Knight.

The Knight has the strangest move of all the pieces. It moves two squares along a rank and then one along a file, or two squares along a file and then one along a rank. The result is a curiously L-shaped move. The Knight can go backward, and it is the only piece that can jump over other men. Diagram 15 shows the Knight's sphere of influence from square c5.

DIAGRAM 15.

19

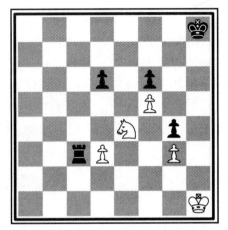

DIAGRAM 16.

QUIZ 5. In Diagram 16, which pieces can the White Knight capture?

The Lowly Pawn

Pawns are the weakest men on the board. They blaze a path for the stronger pieces and often sacrifice themselves for the glory of their army's cause. The pawn's original Sanskrit name was padati. Comparing this word with the Latin word for foot, *pedis*, we can see why the pawn is often likened to a foot soldier. In fact, the Arabic word for the pawn, *baidaq*, means exactly that.

Since the earliest days of chess, the pawn has had the same basic movement: It marches forward one square at a time. The only man that can't move backwards, it is also the only one that captures in a different way than it normally moves: A pawn can capture only by moving one square diagonally. In Diagram 17, the White pawn can capture either the Black Knight or the Black pawn, if the Black pawn doesn't get him first! An enemy pawn can thus be immobilized by placing a pawn or a piece directly in front of it.

When the game was speeded up during the Renaissance, the pawn acquired two dynamic new abilities. The first is relatively straightforward:

If a pawn has never moved, it now has the option of moving either one or two squares forward. It cannot, however, move two squares diagonally for a capture.

Pawn promotion: The second change has much more profound implications. The pawn may seem unimportant, but it is now far from powerless! Like a caterpillar, the pawn dreams of the day when it can metamorphose. All it has to do is amble down the board to the 8th rank (the 1st rank from Black's perspective), and it is immediately promoted to a piece of its own color. It can become a Queen (the usual choice), a Knight, a Bishop, or a Rook; it cannot become a King or remain a pawn. Theoretically, you could have nine Queens on the board at once if all eight of your pawns made it to the last rank! Originally, the pawn could be promoted only to a Minister (the weak original form of the Queen). With the enormous strengthening of the Queen, promoting a pawn to a Queen has become a key strategy in many games.

Diagram 18 shows the sphere of influence of a modern-day pawn from square c5.

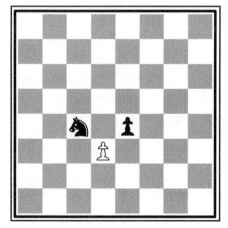

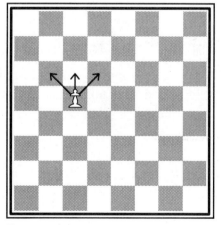

DIAGRAM 17.   **DIAGRAM 18.**

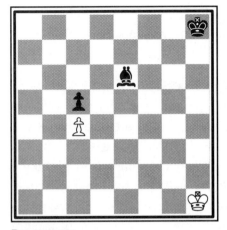

DIAGRAM 19.

DIAGRAM 20.

QUIZ 6. In Diagram 19, can the White pawn move?

QUIZ 7. Find every legal move the White King can make in Diagram 20.

How the Game Is Won

If you attack your opponent's King (called *putting the King in check*) and your opponent is unable to make any move that will prevent you from capturing his King, the result is called *checkmate*. The game is over, and you have won.

Check and Checkmate

The word *checkmate* is derived from the Persian words *shah*, meaning *king*, and *mat*, meaning *helpless* or *defeated*. Being checkmated is, in theory, the only way you can lose a game of chess, but in tournaments players also lose by exceeding time limits or by resigning before a checkmate occurs.

Just 70 years ago, a player was required to announce a check ("Check to your King!"). Today, however, actually saying "Check" is mildly frowned upon, because you might disturb your opponent.

During the game, if your opponent attacks your King you must make every attempt to get your King out of check. You can protect your King in one of three ways:

- ■ Capture the piece that is attacking your King.
- ■ Put something in the way of the enemy piece, thereby blocking the check.
- ■ Move the King to a square that is not under attack.

If your opponent attacks your King and, failing to notice the threat, you move some other piece, your opponent cannot capture your King. You must take your move back and make a different move that gets your King out of check. Not only must you move out of check, but you may not move into check. For that reason, your King must never stand next to your opponent's King.

Diagram 21 shows a check-mated King. The Black King is under attack and has no way to get to safety. Notice that the White Queen is nicely defended by the Bishop on d3.

DIAGRAM 21.

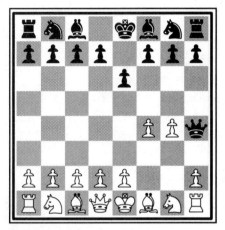

DIAGRAM 22.

QUIZ 8. The position in Diagram 22 came about after the following moves:

1.	f4	e6
2.	g4	Qh4+

How can the White King get out of check?

Capturing: Taking Men Out of Action

I remember playing, as a child, a form of checkers in which the idea was to move your checker next to your opponent's so that he had to capture you, whether he wanted to or not.

Chess is altogether different. If your opponent moves his Queen to a position where you can capture it in five different ways, you should stop and ponder why he would offer you such a valuable gift. If he has indeed made a mistake, snap up that Queen! On the other hand, he may be setting a trap. Perhaps taking his Queen will leave you checkmated! Obviously, you would then want to ignore the Queen altogether and deal with the threat of checkmate. In chess, unlike in checkers, you take only the pieces you want to take.

Aside from a quick checkmate, one of the best ways to win a game is to slowly capture all of your opponent's men, leaving his King defenseless so that you can checkmate with swift brutality. Remember, however, that this strategy works both ways: Be careful that you don't inadvertently allow your opponent to gobble up all your men!

To avoid this kind of humiliation, an experienced player will often choose to resign the game. There are many polite ways to give up. Here are three of them:

- ■ Tip your King over.
- ■ Get on your knees and say, "I give up O Mighty Conquerer." (This obsequious display makes your opponent feel good.)
- ■ Simply say, "I resign."

If you are a beginner, I recommend that you never resign a game. Even in a hopeless position, you can still learn a lesson or two. Closely watch the way your opponent puts you out of your misery. It's just a matter of time before you will get to do it to someone else.

The Confusing Case of Stalemate

One of the more confusing terms to a beginner is that of *stalemate*. A stalemate occurs when one player has no legal moves on the board but

QUIZ 9. In Diagram 23, it is Black's move. Which pieces can he capture?

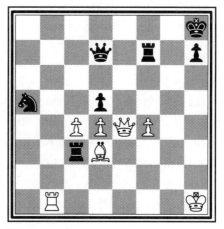

DIAGRAM 23.

25

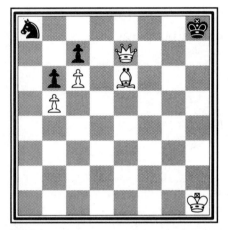

DIAGRAM 24.

must move because it's his turn to do so. This paradox is clearly illustrated in Diagram 24. Black would love to move something but can't! All his pawns are blocked, his Knight is stuck, and his King can't move into danger. When this happens, a stalemate is declared and the game ends as a draw, or a tie.

Though a stalemate has been regarded as a draw since the early 19th century, in England in the 17th and 18th centuries it counted as an "inferior" win. In Middle English, the word *stale* meant *imitation*, so *stalemate* meant *imitation mate*. Modern English language defines the word *stalemate* as a *temporary state of impasse*. But in chess, there's nothing temporary about it. Stalemate ends the game.

Back in the 1600s and 1700s, many players felt that allowing a game to reach a stalemate was dishonorable. In 1614, a chess player by the name of Saul recorded his feelings about stalemates: "You shall understand that a stale is a lost game by him that giveth it, and no question to be made further thereof."

Let's clarify the difference between checkmate and stalemate. In a checkmate, the King is under attack and is unable to get out of danger. In a stalemate, neither the King nor any other piece is able to move, but the King is not being attacked.

The Three Phases of a Chess Game

A game of chess is roughly divided into three phases: the opening, the middlegame, and the endgame.

The opening consists of the first 10 to 15 moves. During this phase, both players bring out their central pawns, quickly mobilizing their Bishops and Knights and castling their Kings.

During the next phase of the game, the middlegame, both players develop long-term, strategical plans and marshall their Rooks and Queens and their minor pieces for attack, counterattack, and defense. If both players survive one another's strategies, the game eventually settles down into an endgame.

The transition from middlegame to endgame is sometimes hard to pinpoint. Endgames generally arise after an exchange of Queens and other major and minor pieces. Typically, endgames are played with a Bishop versus Knight, a Rook versus Rook, or a Rook and a minor piece versus a Rook and a major piece.

As the endgame draws near, the strength of the pawns increases. With fewer pieces to block them, the pawns can move swiftly up the board, like wide receivers in a football game. The strength of the King also increases, and it is able to take an active part in the struggle. Fearful of checks in the opening and middlegame, the King is happy to move out in the open when few pieces are left on the board.

More Moves and Rules

The Enigmatic Rule of En Passant

In the 13th century, if you wanted to move your pawn two squares forward and thus safely bypass an enemy pawn, you could invoke the now-forgotten law of *passar battaglia*, an Italian phrase meaning *to dodge a fight*. Nowadays, this law no longer exists, having been superseded by the last rule to be introduced into modern chess: en passant.

Introduced in the 15th century and mentioned by Ruy López De Segura (c. 1530–c. 1580) in a book written in 1561, en passant was not universally accepted until 1880, when Italian players abandoned the

DIAGRAM 25.

QUIZ 10. In Diagram 25, White should win the game because he is one Queen ahead. Is Qf7 a good move for him here?

passar battaglia law. Even today, en passant is undoubtedly the least known and the most misunderstood of all the rules of chess.

The en passant rule states that if you have a pawn on the 5th rank (the 4th rank from Black's perspective) and an enemy pawn uses its two-square option to move past your pawn, you may capture it as if it had moved only one square. Let's look to Diagram 26 for help.

DIAGRAM 26.

If Black plays his pawn from d7 to d6, then White can capture this pawn by exd6. Realizing this, Black chooses to use his two-square option and moves his pawn from d7 to d5, apparently placing the pawn on a safe square. However, the en passant rule can now kick in, and White can still capture the pawn by exd6 e.p., just as if the pawn had moved to d6 instead of d5!

One important point to note about the en passant rule is that if an enemy pawn moves two squares and goes by you, you must capture it en passant right away or lose the option. If you don't exercise the option, you can still capture another pawn en passant if the opportunity presents itself later in the game. To illustrate this point, let's go back to Diagram 26. Black has just played his pawn from d7 to d5. White chooses not to capture en passant and instead plays his pawn to d4. Now Black plays the pawn on f7 to f5, once again giving White an en passant option. White no longer can capture the d5 pawn but he can play exf6 e.p. if he wants to.

Still confused? Don't panic. You will see helpful examples of this rule later in the book.

QUIZ 11. In Diagram 27, if Black decides not to capture the White pawn on g5 by ...fxg5 and instead plays his pawn to f5, could White then capture the pawn en passant?

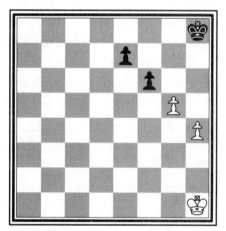

DIAGRAM 27.

The Leap of the King

A composite move of the King and one of the Rooks, castling is the only rule that allows a player to move two pieces at once. Castling is allowed only if you have cleared away all the pieces that stand between the King and the Rook.

There are two types of castling: Kingside and Queenside. In the case of Kingside castling, you simply move your King two squares to the right and place your Rook beside it on the left (see Diagram 28). Queenside castling is the same thing in reverse: You move your King two squares to the left and place your Rook beside it on the right (see Diagram 29).

Firmly established by the 17th century, castling had existed in other forms since the 1300s. Thirteenth-century castling was quite an adventure, with the King able to leap to all sorts of unlikely places. Jacopo Da Cessole states that a King on square e1 could leap to squares c1, c2, c3, d3, e3, f3, g3, g2, and g1, or even to far away b1 or b2. In the 1400s, Luis Ramirez Lucena mentioned castling, but in a form that required two moves to complete. (The Rook was moved first as one move and then the King could leap over to the Rook on the following move.) Ruy López mentioned modern castling in his 1561 book.

Today, castling is an important part of the game. Players usually opt to castle as early as possible in order to place the King in relative safety at the side of the board.

DIAGRAM 28.

DIAGRAM 29.

Here are a few more details:

- If you have moved your King, you can't castle—even if you move the King back to its original square.

- If you have not moved your King but you have moved one of your Rooks, you can castle only on the side of the unmoved Rook.

- You cannot castle if you are in check. You can castle on a subsequent move, but only after you get out of check.

- You cannot castle through check.

In Diagram 30, White cannot castle because his King would move through an attacked square. (Black's Bishop on b5 controls square f1.) Black, on the other hand, can castle. It's perfectly fine for a Rook to pass through an attacked square.

QUIZ 12. Can White castle on either side of Diagram 31?

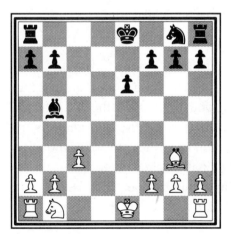

DIAGRAM 30.

DIAGRAM 31.

Gardez!

In the past, custom required that you warn your opponent if you attacked his Queen or Rook. It was not at all unusual to hear a well-mannered gentleman say with great seriousness, "Gardez!"

Though the custom has long since died out, many amateurs are still under the impression that it is proper etiquette to warn an opponent when his Queen is attacked. In fact, if a modern tournament player issued such a warning, he would in turn be warned by the tournament director not to disturb his opponent!

Touch Move and Other Rules

The remaining rules don't apply to amateur chess. For example, according to the touch move rule, if it is your move and you touch a piece, you must move it. In a friendly game, this rule is not really necessary unless both players agree ahead of time to follow it.

Other rules, such as draw by three-time repetition of position (which states that if the identical position occurs three times and each time the same player must move, a draw can be declared), are tournament rules that rarely apply in normal playing situations. Moreover, they have nothing to do with the way the game is actually played.

An Example Game

With all those rules out of the way, we can take a look at an actual game—albeit a short one. For many of you, this may be the first time you have ever played a whole game, so do it carefully. The game is not particularly well played, but it does demonstrate the use of chess notation, the en passant and castling rules, and finally a checkmate.

Work through the following moves, one by one. Then be sure that the positions of the pieces on your board are exactly the same as those in Diagram 32. If they are different, you have made a mistake in following the notation. You should play through the game again to find out where.

1.	e4	e6	8.	O-O	Bd7
2.	d4	d5	9.	b4	cxb3 e.p.
3.	e5	c5	10.	axb3	Rc8
4.	c3	Nc6	11.	Qh5	a6
5.	Bd3	c4	12.	Ng5	g6
6.	Bc2	Nge7	13.	Nxh7	gxh5
7.	Nh3	b6	14.	Nf6 checkmate	

As you can see in Diagram 32, Black has won the White Queen but his King is in check and has nowhere to go! Black is checkmated and has lost the game. Black would have been well-advised to avoid capturing the White Queen and to instead guard against the threatened checkmate.

In the games given in Chapter Six, "Annotated Games," we will discuss each of the moves, mapping out typical opening strategies and exploring the plays that might follow them.

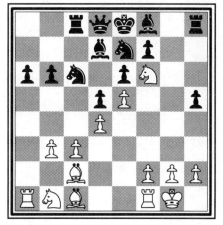

DIAGRAM 32.

Testing Your Skills

Tests help you see how well you have absorbed the information I am giving you. You will find tests sprinkled throughout the chapters. Take as much time as you need and try hard to solve each problem. If some of them give you trouble, don't get upset! Simply look at the solutions at the back of the book and review the chapter that explains that particular concept.

For the first test, assume that these moves have been played:

1.	e4	e5		3.	Nf3	Be7
2.	f4	exf4		4.	Bc4	Bh4+

TEST 1. The White King is under attack. List all the ways he can get out of check.

TEST 2. It is White's turn to play. Hunt down the Black Knight and capture it.

TEST 3. It is White's turn to play. Play for both sides and see whether one side can make a new Queen. Remember, in chess the two sides must move in turn.

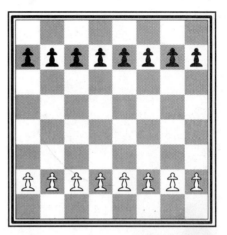

TEST 4. If it is White's turn to play, can he castle on either side? If it is Black's turn to play, can he castle on either side?

TEST 5. It is White's turn to play. List all the pieces that the White Knight on d4 can capture.

TEST 6. Black is trailing by one piece, but he can even the score with the simple capture 1...Nxb4. Is that the best move? Or is there a better one?

TEST 7. Black has only a blocked pawn, and White is tempted by the capturing move 1.Qxf7. Is this a good move?

TEST 8. White is considering the move 1.Rxd7 and also 1.Nd5, which attacks the Black Queen. Is anything wrong with either move?

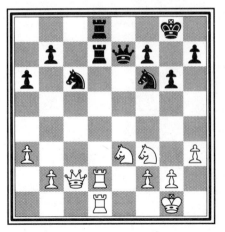

TEST 9. It is Black's turn to play. He would like to move his Rook from f8 to an open file. Which is the better square, d8 or e8?

The First Principle: Force

In chess, the word *force* does not refer to an obscure mystical concept. Nor is the concept of force difficult to understand. When I speak of force, I am referring to the strength of the pieces, either individually or in groups. For example, if you and your opponent have the same pieces on the board and you have one pawn more than your opponent, you have an advantage in force, also known as a *material advantage*.

Gaining a material advantage is one of the best ways to win a game of chess. If you can capture all of your opponent's pieces, his King will be defenseless and your army can easily hunt it down for the big checkmate. If material is even but you have most of your army aimed at the Kingside, whereas your opponent has only a couple of defenders in that sector, then you have an advantage in force on the Kingside. Thus, you can have two kinds of advantages in force:

■ More pieces overall.

■ More pieces in a particular area of the board.

Assigning the Pieces Numerical Values

As a game progresses and pieces are traded or lost, it is not at all unusual for the armies to be left with different types of men. For example, White may have two Rooks, one Bishop, and six pawns, whereas Black may have two Rooks, one Bishop, one Knight, and three pawns. Who is ahead? The easiest way to answer this question is by using a system that assigns a numerical value to each piece. Then you can assess what each army is worth. In order of increasing importance, numerical values are assigned as follows:

- Pawn: 1 point.
- Knight: 3 points.
- Bishop: 3 points.
- Rook: 5 points.
- Queen: 9 points.
- King: Infinite value, because its loss means the loss of the game.

Now we can determine whether White is ahead with two Rooks, one Bishop, and six pawns or whether Black has the edge with two Rooks, one Bishop, one Knight, and three pawns. White's two Rooks are worth 10 points, his Bishop is worth 3 points, and his six pawns are worth 6 points, for a total of 19 points. Black's two Rooks are worth 10 points, his Bishop is worth 3 points, his Knight is worth 3 points, and his three pawns are worth 3 points. Black's grand total is 19 points—exactly the same as White's! We can now see that neither side is materially ahead.

Here are some typical material imbalances:

- A Queen (9 points) versus two Rooks (10 points): The two Rooks are favored.

- A Queen (9 points) and a pawn (1 point) versus a Rook (5 points), a Bishop (3 points), and a Knight (3 points): The side with the Queen has a material disadvantage with 10 points, compared with a total of 11 points for the enemy pieces.

- A Knight (3 points) versus three pawns (3 points): Here, neither side has an advantage.

- A Rook (5 points) and a pawn (1 point) versus a Bishop (3 points) and a Knight (3 points): As far as points go, it's 6 to 6—an even match. However, here is a case in which the numbers may not accurately reflect the true advantage in force. Two minor pieces (remember, Bishops and Knights are minor pieces, not pawns) are usually more active than a Rook and a pawn, especially when many other pieces are on the board. So the two minor pieces are usually considered more valuable.

- A Rook (5 points) versus a Bishop (3 points) and two pawns (2 points): These positions are about equal.

You should now be able to figure out whether trading one of your men for one of your opponent's is favorable to you or to him, at least in terms of force. However, I must warn you against relying too heavily on numbers. Though this table of values is a useful tool, they tend to be more accurate in some types of positions than in others. In one position, three pawns may be superior to a minor piece, whereas in another position, you might well find that a Bishop or Knight completely outweighs three pawns. Thus, after assessing the material advantage in terms of points, you must always take another look at the particular position on the board to see whether it warrants getting involved in the "numbers racket." Use the values as a guide, but use your own eyes as well.

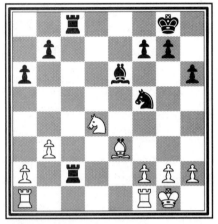

DIAGRAM 33.

QUIZ 13. In Diagram 33, it is White's turn to play. What is his most attractive move?

The Romantic Style of Chess

Though some uninformed people feel that there is only one correct way to play chess, the experienced chess fanatic comes to realize that every player has his or her unique style of play, each as valid as any other. Some players excel in a purely logical approach to chess, breaking each game down and analyzing it with the rigor of scientists. Others rely on delicate maneuvers and subtle positional understanding, imbuing their games with clarity and depth and rendering each game with the artistic flair of classical musicians. The style that has always appealed most to the public, though, is that of the crazed, attacking maniac. This type of player delights in sacrificing his pieces and pawns in an all-out effort to drag down the enemy King as quickly as possible.

An outstanding exponent of this playing style was Frank James Marshall (1877–1944), who held the U.S. Championship from 1909 to 1935. Marshall's daring style often landed him in deep trouble, but fortune smiles on the brave. He was often able to trick his way out of difficulties and, as a result, became known as the *Great Swindler*. The story goes that in one game Marshall sacrificed his Queen in such a

Frank Marshall, the Great Swindler.

shocking way that the audience, enraptured by the beauty of his move, virtually showered him with gold pieces!

How to Gain an Advantage in Force

As I mentioned earlier, there are two kinds of advantages in force: more pieces overall, and more pieces in a particular area of the board. To position more pieces in a particular area of the board, you simply move all your pieces to that sector (usually the Kingside). If your opponent, meanwhile, has moved his pieces elsewhere, you will have an advantage in force in the area where your army is camped.

In Diagram 34, Black's whole army has gone off to smell the roses on the Queenside. White's army stands massed and ready to

DIAGRAM 34.

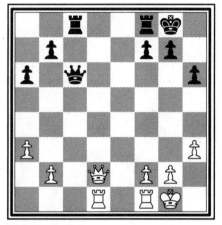

DIAGRAM 35.

DIAGRAM 36.

QUIZ 14. In Diagram 35, it is Black's move. He would like to move his Rook from f8 to an open file. Which is better, ...Rfd8 or ...Rfe8?

QUIZ 15. In Diagram 36, White has his Knight, Rook, and Bishop all aimed at the Kingside and already has an advantage in force there. How can he make that advantage even greater?

destroy the enemy King. White's attack against the Black King will prove successful (the threat of Qxh7 and checkmate is unstoppable), because the poor Black King and his two defending pawns are completely outnumbered.

It's great if you can deploy your men in one area for an attack like this one. It is even better to gain an advantage in force by simply capturing your opponent's pieces. If you succeed, you have a superior army that you can deploy anywhere, secure in the knowledge that your opponent's smaller army cannot match yours. Naturally, your opponent will try hard to prevent you from capturing his pieces, but I'm going to show you some tricks that will often fool even the most experienced players. These tricks, which are officially called *tactics*, include traps, threats, and schemes that are based on the *calculation of variations*. (I discuss the calculation of variations in Chapter Seven, "The Four Principles and You.")

Basic Tactics

We will now examine two basic tactics: the pin and the fork. These tactics are used so often that any student of chess must know them and know them well.

The Pin

The pin is a tactic in which one piece prevents an enemy piece from moving. For example, in Diagram 37 assume that the following moves have been played:

1. e4   e5
2. Nf3   d6
3. Nc3   Bg4

The White Knight on f3 is pinned by the Bishop on g4. This Knight can legally move, but doing so is hardly desirable because it results in the loss of the White Queen—for example, with 4.d4? exd4 5.Nxd4?? Bxd1. Black's material advantage should then lead to

DIAGRAM 37.

eventual victory. Instead of 4.d4?, White would do better to put the question to Black's Bishop by

    4.   h3

because

    4.   ...   Bxf3

    5.   Qxf3

leads to an even trade and ends the pin.

Let's look at another example. The strongest type of pin is the pin against the King. In Diagram 38, the pinned Knight cannot legally move, because doing so exposes the Black King to attack. It is Black's turn to move. The material count is even, and White is attacking the Black Knight. Black's normal reaction would be to simply move the Knight to a safe square. However, he doesn't have that option here, because any Knight move would place the Black King in danger from the White Bishop. Black does not fear Bxc6 because he can retaliate with ...bxc6 (which amounts to an even trade), so he tries to save himself with

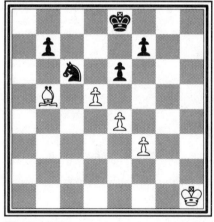

DIAGRAM 38.

    1.   ...   exd5

Now the White pawn is gone, and the Black Knight is adequately protected by the pawn on b7. Unfortunately for Black, however, White answers with

    2.   exd5

renewing the attack on the Knight and threatening to win with 3.dxc6. White's pin has made defense against this threat impossible.

Now let's look at some ways a pin can be used to win material. The position in Diagram 39 came about after these moves:

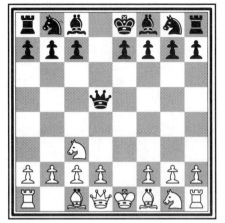

1. e4   d5
2. exd5   Qxd5
3. Nc3

Black must now move his Queen to safety. One of the worst possible moves is to sound a retreat with

3. ...   Qc6??

because White can then play

DIAGRAM 39.

4. Bb5

pinning the Queen to its King and trading the Black Queen (9 points) for the White Bishop (3 points), a gain of 6 points!

Diagram 40 shows another example. Black is doing very well in this position. He is up a Rook (5 points) for a Bishop (3 points) and a pawn (1

point), and it is his turn to play. His best plan would now be to move his King into the action by 1...Kf7 followed by 2...Ke7 and 3...Kd6. Another good idea is to activate the Rook by playing it to the 2nd rank via 1...Rb8 and 2...Rb2. Instead, Black gets greedy and tries to win White's d5-pawn right away by grabbing with

1. ...   Rxd5??

DIAGRAM 40.

DIAGRAM 41.

White counters with

>2.   **Bb3**

The Black Rook is now pinned to his King, unable to get out of danger. After the futile

>2.   ...   **Kf8**

White's response is

>3.   **Bxd5**

White is 3 points ahead and within sight of an easy win.

In Diagram 41, White has a 1-point advantage in force—Bishop and Knight (6 points) versus Rook (5 points)—so things are looking rosy for him. It's Black's turn to play, and his first move is

>1.   ...   **d4**

This attack on the White Bishop also moves the pawn closer to its Queening square. White responds

>2.   **Bxd4??**

White has walked into a trap. If someone offers you a free pawn, always study the board carefully to figure out what trick he has in mind. In this case, White grabbed the pawn without a second thought, only to be slapped in the face with reality. Either 2.Bd2 or 2.Bf4 would have been a better move. After

>2.   ...   **Rd8**

the White Bishop is pinned, because White is unable to move his Bishop without putting his King in checkmate—for example, 3.Bc3 Rd1+ 4.Be1 Rxe1 checkmate. (This type of mate is called a *Back Rank Mate*.) Now White threatens to move his Bishop into safety with

>3.   **g3**

because in response to any Rook check, White's King can then safely step up to g2. Unfortunately, White will not get the opportunity to run away. Black plays

| 3. | ... | Rxd4 |

Now Black is ahead with a 1-point advantage in force—Knight and three pawns (6 points) versus Rook and two pawns (7 points).

The Fork

The second basic tactic, the fork, is a simultaneous attack on two or more pieces by one enemy piece. In fact, forks are often called *double attacks*. Though any piece may perform a fork, the Knight is so adept at this maneuver that it could be called *Mr. Fork*.

In Diagram 42, we can see the horrifying effect of a Knight fork. The Black King is under attack so Black must move it. However, his Queen and Rook are also under fire. Black must give up his Queen (9 points) for

the Knight (3 points). After a rout like this, many beginners come to fear Knights and go out of their way to capture their opponent's horses as fast as possible.

Other examples of forks are given in Tests 10 through 14 at the end of the chapter.

DIAGRAM 42.

49

DIAGRAM 43.

■■■■■■■■■■■■■■

QUIZ 16. In Diagram 43, it is Black's move. Seeing that White threatens to fork him with Nc7+, Black plays

1   ...Bb8+

White answers with

2   Nc7+

blocking Black's check and imposing a check of his own! White feels that after 2...Bxc7+ 3.Rxc7, his Rook will be well placed in the endgame. Was 2.Nc7+ a good move?

Laying Traps

Everyone likes the idea of trapping his opponent. Picture the following: You are in the middle of a long, hard struggle with your nemesis, Pit-Bull Hogan. The game has been even for a long time, when suddenly you seem to have made a grave error! Pit-Bull triumphantly captures your Queen, a snarl on his lips and a triumphant gleam in his eyes. He looks for signs of the panic that he knows you must be feeling. Instead, you calmly make your move and call "Checkmate!"

Doesn't that victory taste sweet? Of course it does! However, I must burst your bubble with a dire warning. Don't play for traps! Always make moves that deploy your men in a way that helps your position generally.

Never play a move that puts you in either of the following emotionally charged situations:

- ■ Your opponent doesn't see your trap and loses horribly.
- ■ He sees your trap and counters in such a way that your position falls apart.

I'm not saying you shouldn't lay a trap, only that you should be sure your position won't be compromised if your opponent avoids the trap.

On occasion, you will find yourself facing an opponent who stumbles into one opening trap after another. On other occasions, your opponent will be the one who is baiting the hook. To successfully trap or avoid being trapped, you must have some familiarity with the basic types of traps: those aimed at weak pawns, those aimed at undefended pieces, and those that batter the King's bodyguards.

A Pair of Weaklings

The first type of trap is based on the weakness of the pawns on squares f7 and f2. In the opening phase of a game, the f7-pawn becomes a major target of White's attack. Black must be very careful that catastrophe does not strike him on that square. Equally, White must be careful about the pawn on square f2. These pawns are particularly vulnerable because they are protected only by Kings, in contrast with the other pawns in front of the Kings. The Black pawns on both d7 and e7, for example, are protected by four pieces. White would like nothing better than to penetrate the line through f7 and launch a major offensive against the enemy monarch.

On the following pages are some typical ways of taking advantage of the weakness of the f7- and f2-pawns.

Scholar's Mate:

1.	e4	e5	3.	Qh5	Nf6??
2.	Bc4	Nc6	4.	Qxf7 checkmate	

Very nice, but what if Black had seen White's threat of checkmate and had taken defensive measures? Instead of 3...Nf6??, Black should have played 3...g6. Then White would play 4.Qf3. (White deserves credit for perseverance! He would once again threaten checkmate on f7.) Then Black would play 4...Nf6 and, in-stead of the result shown in Dia-gram 44, all would be well.

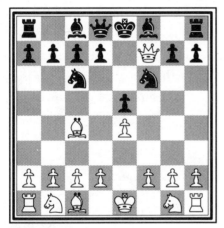

DIAGRAM 44.

I can't recommend the Scholar's Mate tactic, because if Black sees the threat (and he usually will), the White Queen will have developed too early and will, as a result, lose time as it runs away from Black's pieces. This concept is discussed in more detail in Chapter Three, "The Second Principle: Time."

Legall's Mate:

1.	e4	e5	3.	Nc3	g6
2.	Nf3	d6	4.	Bc4	Bg4?

Black has tied down White's Knight on f3 with a pin. However, his Bishop is undefended on g4 and White's army is better developed. White can now launch a surprise attack against square f7.

5.   Nxe5!!

White seems to have gone berserk!

Black should now limit his losses and play 5...dxe5, to which White would respond 6.Qxg4. However, instead of losing a pawn, Black eats White's Queen—as most people would:

5. ... Bxd1?

So Black captures a Queen. But now Black's pawn on f7 falls and White's attack crashes through:

6. Bxf7+ Ke7

7. Nd5 checkmate

DIAGRAM 45.

As Diagram 45 shows, Black ate too much and got heartburn.

The Case of the Undefended Piece

The second type of trap is known as a *discovery*, or a *discovered attack*. Discovered attacks are usually directed at undefended pieces. Any undefended piece is subject to loss and must be carefully watched. Some examples of ways to use undefended pieces for setting traps include the following.

The Excommunicated Bishop:

1.	e4	e5	4.	Nc3	Bg4
2.	Nf3	d6	5.	O-O	
3.	Bc4	Nc6			

The Legall's Mate move, 5.Nxe5, would not work here because Black can play 5...Nxe5! to prevent the checkmate and defend the Bishop on g4.

DIAGRAM 46.

Next, Black plays

| 5. | ... | Nge7?? |

He would do better to play 5...Nf6, simply defending the Bishop on g4.

| 6. | Bxf7+! | Kxf7 |
| 7. | Ng5+ | |

The Knight checks, thereby uncovering a Queen attack on the Black Bishop—a perfect example of a discovered attack.

| 7. | ... | Ke8 |
| 8. | Qxg4 | |

White has now gained a pawn. The final position is shown in Diagram 46.

When you first start playing chess, you should be very careful about snatching pawns in the opening. Your Queen can often get caught dipping her hand into the cookie jar, as you'll see in the next example.

The Queen That Never Came Home:

1.	e4	d5		4.	d4	e6
2.	exd5	Qxd5		5.	Bd3	Qxd4??
3.	Nc3	Qd8				

Black thinks that White has overlooked a pawn but a surprise is in store.

| 6. | Bb5+! | |

As you can see in Diagram 47, White has initiated a discovered attack on Black's Queen. Because Black is in check, he can do nothing to defend the Queen. Note that 6...Nc6 would not help, because after 7.Qxd4, the Black Knight would be pinned by the Bishop to his King and would be unable to make a capture.

Discovered attacks on far-flung pieces are common traps, and you need to understand them completely in order to foil them. At this point, though, you should concentrate on recognizing the danger of allowing an advancing piece to go undefended.

The Battering Ram

The final type of trap is based on dismantling the enemy King's cover, otherwise known as *playing for a devastating check*. Having the skills to blaze a trail to the enemy King is important. Sometimes, however, your opponent cooperates before you can display your skills. Probably the most famous example of an opened-up King is the Fool's Mate.

Fool's Mate:

1.   f4

This move is called the *Bird Opening*.

1.   ...   e6
2.   g4??

For no reason whatsoever White has opened up his own King to attack on the e1-h4 diagonal.

2.   ...   **Qh4 checkmate**

Diagram 48 shows the horrifying result.

DIAGRAM 47.

DIAGRAM 48.

Let's look at another example of how you can blast through the enemy's defenses:

1.	f4	e5
2.	fxe5	

With this second move, White avoids 2.g3 exf4 3.gxf4?? Qh4 checkmate.

2.	...	d6

Black is not tempted by 2...Qh4+, which would be adequately countered by 3.g3, when Black's Queen must retreat.

3.	exd6	Bxd6

Black has sacrificed a pawn so that he can obtain a lead in development. This type of deliberate sacrifice in the opening is called a *gambit*.

4.	Nc3??	

Oops. White didn't see the threat. He should have played 4.Nf3, which would develop a piece and prevent ...Qh4+, Black's next move.

DIAGRAM 49.

4.	...	Qh4+
5.	g3	Qxg3+!!
6.	hxg3	Bxg3 checkmate

The final position is shown in Diagram 49. It should now be clear to you why the King is not safe in his starting position and why I recommend that you castle as quickly as possible.

There is one more type of trap I'd like you to look at.

The Cheap Check:

1.	e4	c6		4.	Nxe4	Nd7
2.	d4	d5		5.	Qe2	Ngf6
3.	Nc3	dxe4		6.	Nd6 checkmate	

As you can see in Diagram 50, the Black King has no way to get out of check, and he cannot capture the rude Knight because the pawn on e7 is pinned by the White Queen. This maneuver is called a *Smothered Mate*. Looks great, doesn't it? Why, then, do I call it a cheap check? Because if Black sees the threat, White's fifth move (Qe2) would prove to be a liability. Let's say that after 5.Qe2 Black says to himself, "Aha! I see what he's up to. I won't let him do that to me!" Black then plays 5...Ndf6 while his Queen guards square d6 and unveils an attack against the d4-pawn.

QUIZ 17. In Diagram 51, it is White's turn to move. He is tempted to play 1.Nc4 in spite of the strong threat of 2.Nd6 checkmate. Is this a good move?

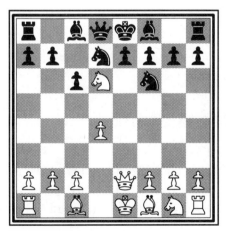

DIAGRAM 50.

DIAGRAM 51.

The defects of White's fifth move are then clear: White has taken a defender away from d4 and blocked his Bishop on f1. The moral: Never make a move with the thought, "I hope he doesn't see it."

The King Plays in the Endgame

Having played all the crushing checkmates described in the preceding pages, you understand why players castle quickly and hide their Kings. All the hard work is left to the rest of the army. Unless your opponent attacks your King, it becomes easy to forget that you even have one.

In the first two phases of a game (the opening and the middlegame), the King is for the most part a liability. However, in the third phase (the endgame), the King takes its place as a fighting piece of great power. Sensing that victory is near, the King steps out of hiding and leads its remaining army in its last battle. It finally adopts the mantle of responsibility. How can the King afford to step out? Why is the King now safe?

Though beginners may feel intimidated by the endgame, in top-flight chess endgame skill is very important, and players take every opportunity to cultivate it. The endgame is a phase in which most of the pieces have been lost or traded. It stands to reason that once the board has been cleared of King-eating piranhas, his majesty can safely take a stroll. The King is particularly safe when only pawns are left. So it pays to always keep in mind that the King is a powerful piece and that you should bring the King into play as soon as you can safely do so.

Material Advantage in the Endgame

It's late at night. You've been sitting at the same board for hours, but you know it's all going to be worthwhile. You are playing your archenemy and the game has been going very well for you. Even though your opponent has traded virtually all his pieces, you are still a whole Queen ahead. "This should be easy," you think. Frustration, however, is going to be your midnight snack tonight. It turns out that no matter what you do, you just can't checkmate his King.

It happens all the time. It's no use playing a good opening and gaining a material advantage in the middlegame if you don't know how to win from there! With just two endgame strategies up your sleeve, you should be able to win almost every game if you are ahead by a Rook or more. These strategies are of great importance simply because the circumstances under which you can use them occur so often. I recommend that you make an effort to learn them as thoroughly as possible.

The two endgames are:

■ King and Queen versus lone King.

■ King and Rook versus lone King.

King and Queen versus Lone King

With practice, the endgame strategy I'm about to describe will become easy for you, but only if you bear in mind two important facts:

■ White cannot checkmate Black with the White Queen alone. White's King must trek across the board and assist in the execution.

■ Checkmate with a King and Queen can be accomplished only at the board's edge.

From Diagram 52, White proceeds with the endgame as follows:

1.   Qb5

DIAGRAM 52.

59

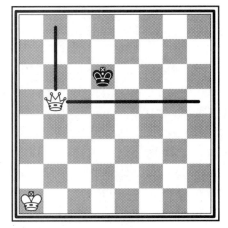

DIAGRAM 53.

With this move, White is trapping the Black King in a "box" (see Diagram 53).

The box method of checkmating is easiest, though slightly faster methods are also possible. The strategy here is to make the box smaller and smaller. After White's Queen has trapped the Black King on the back rank, White's King will march over and assist the Queen as it delivers the death blow.

Meanwhile, Black is still struggling to find a way out:

| 1. | ... | Ke6 |

If Black plays 1...Kc7, White tightens the noose with 2.Qa6. In this case, White plays

| 2. | Qc5 |

and squeezes Black a bit more. White avoided playing 2.Qc6+?, because a response of 2...Ke5 from Black would allow the Black King more room. Instead, Black plays

| 2. | ... | Kf6 |

Other possible moves are 2...Kd7 and 3.Qb6, both of which lead to the same type of play. White's response is

| 3. | Qd5 |

Notice that White does not lose track of his goals by uselessly checking his opponent. Instead, he calmly continues with his space-gaining strategy. There is nothing Black can do. He must give ground.

| 3. | ... | Kg6 |

White could move his King up at any time, but he continues the Queen's siege:

4.   Qe5

And Black continues the King's retreat:

4.   ...   Kf7

If Black plays 4...Kh6, White would play 5.Qg3, thus trapping the Black King on the edge of the board. Then White would march his King to f6 and checkmate would follow. In this case, however, White plays

5.   Qd6

Now Black is trapped on the last two ranks:

5.   ...   Kg7

He is rapidly running out of breathing room.

6.   Qe6

Black is now forced to go to the edge of the board.

6.   ...   Kh7

If Black plays 6...Kf8, White would respond 7.Qd7, which would then lead to the same type of play.

7.   Qg4

As Diagram 54 shows, White has achieved the first part of his goal and the Black King is trapped on the side of the board. Now that Black is completely helpless (he can move his King only to h6, h7, or h8), White can quietly move his King across the board to square f6.

7.   ...   Kh6

8.   Kb2

DIAGRAM 54.

As the King finally starts on its journey, Black plays his only legal move.

| 8. | ... | Kh7 | | 10. | Kd4 |
| 9. | Kc3 | Kh8 | | | |

White must be very careful to avoid a stalemate. For example, 10.Qg6?? would have put a smile on Black's face.

| 10. | ... | Kh7 | | 12. | Kf6 | Kh7 |
| 11. | Ke5 | Kh8 | | 13. | Qg7 checkmate | |

Practice this endgame as often as you can, and you will find that you'll master it quickly. Remember, the goal of this simple technique is to avoid useless checks and drive your opponent's King to the edge of the board.

King and Rook versus Lone King

Because the Rook is weaker than the Queen, it stands to reason that a King–Rook alliance will have more difficulty achieving a checkmate. As with the previous example, White must drive the Black King to the edge of the board. In this case, however, the task can only be carried out with the combined efforts of both the King and the Rook.

Diagram 55 shows the starting positions. White makes his move:

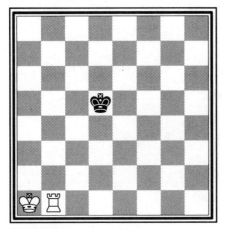

DIAGRAM 55.

| 1. | Kb2 |

Here are a couple of basic principles to keep in mind: White should move his King as close as possible to the Black King (one square apart) and only then should he use his Rook; and Black should try to keep his King in the middle of the board, because it is impossible for White to checkmate him there.

| 1. | ... | Kd4 |

An inferior move is 1...Kc4, to which White would respond 2.Rd1!, trapping the Black King on the a-, b-, and c-files. In this case, White plays

2.   Kc2

Note how the White King is taking squares c3 and d3 away from his Black counterpart.

2.   ...   Ke4

Once again, 2...Kc4 would have been met by 3.Rd1, and the Black King would have lost ground faster than necessary. White continues pushing Black back with his King.

3.   Kc3   Ke5

Another possibility for Black is 3...Ke3, though this move would make White's task somewhat easier by setting up the sequence 4.Re1+ Kf2 5.Re4 Kf3 6.Kd3. As things are, White's King is positioned just as well as Black's, and it's time for the White Rook to join in the fight.

4.   Kc4   Ke4

If Black played 4...Ke6, White would cut off the Black King with 5.Rb5. Here, White plays

5.   Re1+

A Rook check is always strong when the Kings face off, because the checked King is thereby forced to relinquish ground.

5.   ...   Kf5

An interesting moment: White would like to have the Kings face off as they did a move ago. However, if White plays 6.Kd5, Black could slip away from the face-off with 6...Kf4.

6.   Kd4

By playing his King to d4, White invites Black to step into a face-off with 6...Kf4 so that White can play 7.Rf1+ and keep forcing Black toward

DIAGRAM 56.

the edge of the board (see Diagram 56). The following moves would be 7...Kg5 8.Ke4 Kg6 9.Ke5 Kg5 10.Rg1+ Kh4 11.Kf5 (as before, the White King would avoid facing off with the Black King, waiting for Black to step into the face-off) 11...Kh3 (Black would have no choice, because 11...Kh5 12.Rh1 is checkmate) 12.Kf4 Kh2 13.Rg3 (making a cage) 13...Kh1 14.Kf3 Kh2 15.Kf2 Kh1 16.Rh3 checkmate.

White must avoid 16.Rg2??, which would result in a draw by stalemate.

However, Black ignores the invitation and avoids the face-off:

DIAGRAM 57.

6.	...	Kf6
7.	Re5	

Black is now caught in the small cage shown in Diagram 57, but he keeps on struggling:

7.	...	Kg6

White hastens to get his King closer to Black's:

8.	Ke4	Kf6
9.	Kf4	

White must avoid the hasty 9.Rf5+?, which allows Ke6 and increases Black's ability to scamper.

    9.   ...   Kf7

The cage would also get smaller with 9...Kg6 10.Rf5.

    10. Kf5

The White King has taken squares f6 and g6 away from the Black King.

    10. ...   Kg7

    11. Re7+

The Black King has been successfully forced to the side of the board. However, the only way that White can put the Black King in checkmate is to force the Kings to face off. Then a Rook check will produce checkmate, because the Black King will be unable to go backward or forward without moving into the White King's sphere of control. Black's only hope is to avoid the face-off with

    11. ...   Kf8

A worse move is 11...Kh6, because White would not play 12.Kf6?, leading to 12...Kh5 13.Kf5 Kh4. After 11...Kh6, White would simply waste a move with 12.Rd7 (12.Rf7 or anywhere else along the 7th rank would be just as good), and Black would be forced to move his King into the unwanted face-off situation with 12...Kh5. After White has achieved the face-off, 13.Rh7 would be checkmate.

    12. Kf6   Kg8

    13. Kg6   Kf8

Black obviously does not want his King to be in front of the White King. White now steps back a bit and forces Black to walk toward his doom:

    14. Re6   Kg8

    15. Re8 checkmate

The King–Rook maneuver may seem difficult at first, but the combination occurs often. Take a little time to master it, and your nights of frustration will become evenings of glee!

DIAGRAM 58.

QUIZ 18. In Diagram 58, can the White King and Bishop win? Could White win if you replaced the Bishop with a Knight?

Preference or Principle: A Fine Line

By now, you know that a Rook has more force than a Knight and that a Bishop has more force than a pawn. However, you must keep your mind open enough to recognize situations in which you should bend these principles.

David Janowski, the stubborn Grandmaster.

It is not at all unusual for players to become infatuated with a particular aspect of the game and to make a point of playing for it in one contest after another, usually to their detriment. One example of this type of mania was seen in the Grandmaster David Janowski (1868–1927). Frank Marshall, a good friend of Janowski, wrote: "He

66

had little foibles about the kind of game he liked—his weakness for the two Bishops was notorious—and he could be tremendously stubborn. Janowski could follow the wrong path with more determination than any man I met! He was also something of a dandy and quite vain about his appearance."

Janowski loved playing with two Bishops. This love became a liability because his opponents learned to offer him the two Bishops, but only at considerable cost in terms of his other pieces! Giving in to temptation led Janowski to make mistakes, while resisting temptation was frustrating for the lover of the Bishops. It is small wonder that U.S. players for many years called the two Bishops *the two Jans*.

When Less Is More

In many instances in chess, a weaker piece proves to have more force than a piece with greater numerical value. Diagram 59 is a case in point. White is to play. If it were Black's move, or if the pawn were on any square other than b7 or d7, White would have a losing position. But here, the pawn is better than the Rook. That news should come as only a small surprise. The big surprise is that after 1.dxc8, White will do better to promote the pawn to a Rook than to a Queen, because after 1.dxc8=Q, Black is stalemated. (Promotion to anything other than a Queen is a tactic called *underpromotion*.) Promoting the pawn to a Rook allows 1...Kb7, resulting in one of the endgames that you have just learned how to win. Try playing through the moves for practice.

DIAGRAM 59.

67

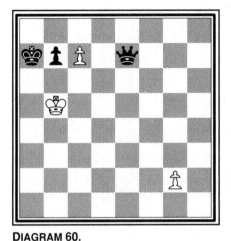

DIAGRAM 60.

Generalities are useful in chess. However, the specifics of a position determine whether a particular principle applies. Diagram 60 shows another example of underpromotion. Here, Black is a Queen ahead, but it is White's turn to move. White can promote his pawn to a Queen, thereby regaining material equality. Instead, White promotes to the numerically inferior Knight, calling check and forking Black's King and Queen. After 1.c8=N+ Kb8 2.Nxe7, White is left with an extra Knight. He promotes his other pawn to a Queen, and the win is easy.

Tests

TEST 10. It is Black's move and he would like to get the Knight on f8 into the game. He is considering 1...Ne6 and 1...Ng6. Which move would you choose?

TEST 11. It is White's turn to play. What is White's best move here?

TEST 12. It is Black's turn to play. What is Black's best move?

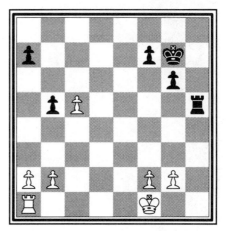

TEST 13. It is White's turn to play. What is White's best move?

TEST 14. It is Black's move. What would you do in Black's position?

The Second Principle: Time

I n this chapter, I'm going to talk about the second principle of chess, time. Though some chess games are timed (see "Chess Timers" in Chapter One, "The Evolution of Chess"), the second principle has nothing to do with clocks. An advantage in time denotes a situation in which you can bring your pieces to a particular part of the board faster than your opponent can.

Think about it. Would you rather have your forces huddled on their starting squares or have them mobilized in the middle of the board, ready to charge to any needy area?

Let's put it another way: You are fighting a battle on Mars. If your forces are still on Earth, you can expect to lose the battle by default. On the other hand, if your army is just a few thousand miles away, then you can expect to arrive at the scene in time. Proximity immeasurably increases your chances for victory.

Time in Action

In many ways, the concepts of time and force are similar. Having a time advantage usually means that you have enough force available to stop an enemy assault.

DIAGRAM 61.

In Diagram 61, Black's army is nicely mobilized. His Rook on c8 controls the c-file, while his Bishop and Queen eye the Queenside. It is White's turn to move. White might decide to launch a Kingside attack by 1.Ng5, threatening Qxh7 checkmate. Can Black defend himself?

Black can successfully stop White's threat of checkmate because he has time to bring defenders to the Kingside. Note that whereas White has only his Queen and the Knight on g5 to attack with, Black can defend with his pawns on f7, g7, and h7, his Bishop on d7, his Rook on f8, and his Knights on e7 and e8. Additionally, Black's King defends the pawns on h7, g7, and f7, as well as the Rook on f8. After 1.Ng5, Black can stop the checkmate with either 1...h6 (which also attacks the White Knight) or 1...Nf6 (which guards h7 and attacks the White Queen). This latter move gains time because it forces White to move his Queen out of danger. If White plays 2.Qh4, then 2...Ng6 brings another Black piece to the Kingside and attacks the White Queen again—resulting in another gain of time as White is forced to get his Queen out of danger.

Obviously, White's Kingside attack never has a chance, because he is outgunned on the Kingside. By gaining time with threats to the White Queen, Black is able to marshall a Kingside defense. White's attacking pieces will be routed.

A time advantage can also refer to an advantage in force that enables your men to blast through your opponent's defenses. Take a look at Diagram 62. Look familiar? The principal difference between this diagram and Diagram 61 is that both the h-pawns are gone. Black no longer has the

DIAGRAM 62.

DIAGRAM 63.

defensive pawn on h7 and White's Rook is no longer blocked by the pawn on h2. As a result, the White Rook joins the attack. The fact that White has gained an important attacker while Black has lost an important defender gives White a winning advantage. After 1.Qh5, the dual threats of 2.Qh7+ and 2.Qh8+ will lead to checkmate.

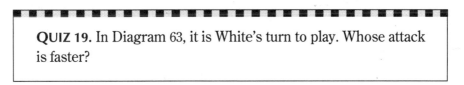

QUIZ 19. In Diagram 63, it is White's turn to play. Whose attack is faster?

The Attack of the Berserker

Beginning chess players tend to want to checkmate their opponent as quickly as possible. Like berserkers—ancient Scandinavian warriors who worked themselves up into battle frenzies—they often move out two pieces and charge the enemy position. If the assault results in checkmate, then well and good. If their opponent fends off the attacking pieces, capturing them or pushing them back to their own territory, then likely as not, berserkers will bring out two more men and charge again. Waves of attack continue until one side or the other wins the game.

The berserker will lose many games until he realizes that two men are rarely enough to overpower the whole enemy army. Don't be a berserker. Instead, get all your pieces out and go after your opponent with *everything* you've got.

Development:
One Key to a Time Advantage

Development—the process of moving one's pieces from their starting posts to new and more effective positions—is an extremely important way to measure time. Let's have a look at the first few moves of a typical opening:

1.   e4

White's move controls the important d5 central square and frees the Queen and f1-Bishop.

1.   ...   e5

Black is also fighting for the center! He puts pressure on square d4 and frees his f8-Bishop and Queen.

2.   Nf3

White develops a Knight. On g1, the Knight threatened nothing and controlled only three squares (e2, f3, and h3). Now the Knight counters Black's control of square d4, attacks Black's e5-pawn, and has eight squares (e1, g1, h2, h4, g5, e5, d4, and d2) within its sphere of control. Without a doubt, White has improved the position of this Knight.

2.   ...   Nc6

Black also develops his Knight. It previously controlled only squares a6, c6, and d7. Now it eyes eight squares: b8, d8, e7, e5, d4, b4, a5, and a7.

Black continues to put pressure on the d4 central square and also guards his e5-pawn!

3.   Bc4

White increases the sphere of control of this Bishop from five squares—e2, d3, c4, b5, and a6—to a hefty ten squares—f1, e2, d3, b5, a6, a2, b3, d5, e6, and f7. (Remember, a piece is not considered to control the square it sits on.) White also continues to fight for the center by jabbing at d5. Other virtues of the 3.Bc4 move: It makes Black's King uncomfortable because the Bishop is now eyeing the delicate f7-pawn, and it allows White to castle on his next move if he wants to.

3.   ...   Bc5

Black also makes his Bishop stronger, and he puts a third man on the d4 brigade. (The Knight on c6, the pawn on e5, and the Bishop on c5 all attack square d4.) Black intends to move the g8-Knight so that he can clear the back rank and castle. Note how both sides have avoided moving their Queens so that other pieces cannot attack them and gain time.

So far, both sides have moved logically, steering undeveloped pieces toward the center. They will not consider launching an attack until their Kings are safely castled and the rest of their men have been brought out. What if White now moved his c4-Bishop again, playing 4.Be2? Is that a good move? No. It is weak, because it moves an already developed piece when other men are begging to be brought into the fight!

One Move per Piece

This brings us to a very useful principle:

Don't move a piece twice in the opening.

Only when all your pieces are developed should you move one of them a second time, in an effort to build up a decisive attack. When you move the same piece twice in the opening, you lose time. To White's move of

DIAGRAM 64.

4.Be2, Black would reply 4...Nf6. As Diagram 64 shows, Black would then have brought out three pieces (not counting his pawns) to White's two!

This gaff is called *losing a tempo* (one unit of time—the plural is *tempi*). You should make every effort to avoid situations that lead to the loss of tempi. The following game example should be enough to serve as a warning to those of you who may be feeling that the loss of a tempo or two is unimportant and hardly worth worrying about:

1.   e4   d5

Black's move is called the *Center Counter Defense*. Though it attacks White's pawn on e4 and frees the Queen and the c8-Bishop, this move is generally considered inferior because it leads to a loss of time. Next, White plays

2.   exd5

Is he violating the principle of not moving a piece twice in the opening? Yes, but in this case White has a good reason. By capturing Black's pawn, White temporarily wins material (a pawn is 1 point). Not wanting to be behind in material so early in the game, Black will also move to capture a pawn, thereby violating the principle of not bringing out the Queen too early! With the early development of Black's Queen, White will regain the loss of time that resulted from moving his pawn twice.

2.   ...   Qxd5

The material balance is once again even.

3.   Nc3

White's Knight moves to a nice central post, from which it controls the e4 and d5 squares and increases its own radius of power. White also gains time by attacking the Black Queen, which must move again. You see now why you should not develop a Queen too early.

Black's reaction is

3.   ...   Qe5+?

Black thinks he is attacking with his Queen. Though a check is always tempting, leaving the Queen in the center leads to a further loss of time. A safer square for the Black Queen would have been a5, where White's pieces could not immediately attack her. White plays

4.   Be2

stopping the check and developing the Bishop.

4.   ...   Nc6

Black has finally developed a second piece! White does not give him time to do it again:

5.   Nf3

With this move, White brings out another piece and gains more time, because Black's Queen is now under fire. Black responds with another horrible move:

5.   ...   Qc5?

He had to move his Queen, but he should have made an effort to get away from the White pieces. 5...Qa5 was called for, but even this move leaves Black way behind in development.

6.   d4

White gains more time by another attack on the poor Black Queen! Moreover, the pawn move is worthwhile because it helps to control the e5 central square and frees the c1-Bishop.

6.   ...   Qd6

7.   Nb5!

With such a big lead in development, White can justify moving the same piece twice. Anyway, this play does not result in a loss of tempo, because Black must once again move his tormented Queen:

    7.   ...   Qb4+

Black tries to find sanctuary in a check. A quiet move like 7...Qd8 would have allowed 8.Bf4, developing the White Bishop to an aggressive post. The attack on the c7-pawn would then leave Black helpless to prevent a loss of material. White plays

    8.   Bd2

A move like 8.c3 would also stop the check, but White consistently, and correctly, brings another piece—rather than a pawn—into play.

    8.   ...   Qxb2

Black takes a pawn, miserably opening the way for 9.Nxc7+ followed by 10.Nxa8. White declines the easy win and instead opts to heap more indignities upon the Black Queen:

    9.   Bc3!

As you can see in Diagram 65, the Queen is now trapped. White's whole army is ready for battle, while the lazy Black forces are still asleep at home. Black gives up, or, in official terms, he resigns.

Going for a Gambit

At times, one side (more often White) opens the game with a gambit. A gambit is a voluntary sacrifice of a piece or pawn in the opening, with the idea of a lead in development and a subsequent attack as compensation.

DIAGRAM 65.

Let's have a look at a common gambit.

  1. e4   e5
  2. d4

Having freed the f1-Bishop with his first move, White now frees his other Bishop. The threat of dxe5 and the loss of a pawn forces Black to react:

  2. ...   exd4

Black has moved his pawn twice in the opening, hoping that White will now play 3.Qxd4 so that he can respond with 3...Nc6, thereby developing a piece and attacking the White Queen. This strategy would gain time for Black, because White would be forced to move his Queen a second time. However, White has no intention of regaining his lost material:

  3. c3!?

Black now moves the pawn a third time!

  3. ...   dxc3

Black feels compelled to prevent White from capturing the pawn with cxd4. He is obviously breaking the rules. However, White is also going against conventional wisdom by losing material right at the beginning of the game!

  4. Bc4

White ignores the impudent pawn and instead rushes to develop his pieces as quickly as possible.

  4. ...   cxb2

Black moves the pawn a fourth time! However, this move makes sense. Even if White captures the pawn, Black will still be two points ahead.

  5. Bxb2

Now White must take the pawn or the pawn will capture the Rook on a1 and turn into a Queen!

DIAGRAM 66.   **DIAGRAM 67.**

Let's summarize this position (see Diagram 66). White has a substantial lead in development. He hopes to use that lead to blow Black off the board. For his part, Black is two pawns (2 points) ahead. If he can now develop his pieces and catch up with White's development, Black will have a free-and-clear material advantage.

As is typical of such gambits, the battle will rage fiercely for the next few moves. White will try hard to pick a fight and kill Black by dint of superior mobilization. Black will ignore White's provocations as much as possible and get his forces out as quickly as he can. A tough and interesting battle will result. You'll find typical plays for similar gambit positions in Chapter Six, "Annotated Games."

QUIZ 20. In Diagram 67, it is Black's move. He is already a pawn ahead and is just dying to eat the White pawn on a2. Would capturing the pawn be a good idea?

Discovering Positional Chess

In the early 1800s, people played chess in one of two simple ways: Either they attacked or they defended. The year 1857 saw the unveiling of a new strategy. That was the year that Paul Morphy (1837–84) of New Orleans won the first American Chess Congress. On the strength of that success, he decided to go to Europe to challenge the world's greatest players. One year later, he had defeated everyone who was brave enough to accept his challenge. Clearly the best player in the world, he returned home to New Orleans and retired from chess. In his final years, he withdrew from society and suffered delusions of persecution. He would eat food prepared only by his mother, and at night he would form a large circle on the ground with women's shoes and dance around them! He died of a stroke at age 47, while taking a bath.

What made Morphy a superior chess player? Morphy was the first player to appreciate the value of development. While his opponents would bring out two or three pieces and start a berserker-style attack, Morphy would quietly defend against their threats, develop his whole army, and then shatter their defenses with his greater force.

Paul Morphy, development genius.

Using a Time Advantage

An advantage in development is only a temporary advantage. If, after developing all your pieces, you find yourself with a lead in development, you must attack with great verve and try to make use of the superior force at your disposal.

In Diagram 68, Black has a terrible position. His King is still in the center and most of his army is sitting at home. White, on the other hand,

DIAGRAM 68.

has done everything right. His King is safely castled, and, as a result, he is able to use his Rook to guard his strong, cramping (restricting) center pawn on e5. All of White's army is developed and is fighting for the critical central squares.

Because of his enormous lead in development, White should try to burst through Black's pawn position and get at the Black King. In line with this strategy, White charges into enemy territory, secure in the knowledge that the greater force he can mobilize should prove decisive:

1. Ng5!

White threatens to win a pawn by 2.Nxh7 (the Bishop on d3 would guard the Knight) or 2.Qf3. Black will have difficulty defending his pawn on f7. Here's one possible play sequence: 1...h5? (which guards the h7-pawn but wastes time and gives White a free hand to do anything else that crosses his mind) 2.Qf3 Nf5 (2...f6 3.Nxe6 would cost the lady) 3.Bxf5 exf5 4.exd6+ (discovered check by the Rook on e1) and Black is dead.

This scenario shows what can happen when a Rook comes into play down an open file. (An open file is one that is free of pawns.) Rooks *love* open files. Position your Rooks on open files and watch your opponent's position fry!

Black tries an alternative play:

1. **...** **h6**

A logical move. Black gets his pawn out of danger and gains time by attacking the White Knight on g5. Under normal circumstances, this move might prove effective, but White's lead in development is so great that White's army manages to come crashing through:

2. **Nxe6!!**

As you can see in Diagram 69, White is offering up a sacrifice in order to tear down the protective wall around Black's King. Though White will lose his Knight (3 points) for a mere pawn (1 point), he feels that opening up the Black King will eventually enable him to checkmate it. Because the King has an unlimited value, sacrificing a Knight (and any number of other pieces) for a King always turns out to be a great trade! Black has no choice but to accept the offering:

2. **...** **fxe6**

White threatens to capture the Black Queen with his Knight, so the rude horse must be taken out of action. White responds with

3. **Qh5+**

Notice how all of White's moves are forcing moves. By playing in this fashion, White denies Black the option of developing more of his

DIAGRAM 69.

83

DIAGRAM 70.

pieces. Instead, Black is reduced to reacting to White's threats.

    3.   **...**   **g6**

Forced (3...Ng6 loses the Knight).

    4.   **Bxg6+**   **Nxg6**

    5.   **Qxg6+**   **Ke7**

Do you see how White can win from this position? Take some time to study Diagram 70 and try to figure out the plays.

    6.   **exd6+**

This move blasts open the e-file and allows the White Rook on e1 to join in the attack. This *teamwork* is an important concept. White's attack is successful because he has many pieces that can work together to bully the Black King. (An even prettier way of opening the e-file would be the sacrifice 6.Nd5+!! exd5 7.exd6 double check and checkmate! Notice how strong a double check can be. White would attack the Black King with both his Rook and the d6-pawn. Such a double attack often allows no escape.)

    6.   **...**   **Kxd6**

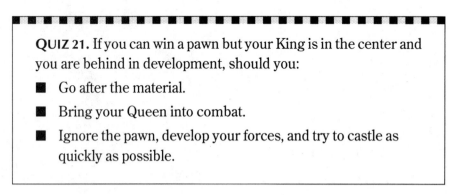

QUIZ 21. If you can win a pawn but your King is in the center and you are behind in development, should you:

- ■ Go after the material.
- ■ Bring your Queen into combat.
- ■ Ignore the pawn, develop your forces, and try to castle as quickly as possible.

If Black plays 6...cxd6 instead, White would have the pleasant choice between 7.Qxe6 checkmate or 7.Nd5 checkmate. The latter is possible because of the pin on the e-pawn by the Rook on e1. As it is, White can still deliver the death blow:

7.   Rxe6 checkmate

Mission accomplished. The King is dead; long live the King!

Tests

TEST 15. It is White's turn to play. White wants to attack the Black King, so he plays 1.Qf3. Should Black be concerned with White's attack?

TEST 16. This is the position after 1.e3 e5 2.Qh5 (attacking the e5-pawn) 2...Nc6 3.Bc4. White is already attacking and threatens to win right away with 4.Qxf7 checkmate. Is it time for Black to panic?

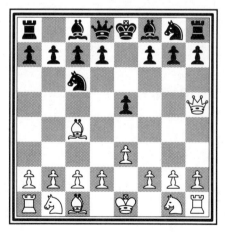

The Third Principle: Space

S o far, I have discussed winning by vicious attacks and winning by the more mundane (but highly effective) method of simply capturing all your opponent's pieces. Now it's time to address another method: squeezing your opponent to death. To squeeze an opponent, you must first acquire a significant advantage in space.

When you have an advantage in space, you control more territory than your opponent. Your pieces have more squares to choose from than the enemy pieces, which are severely restricted in their movements. By applying the principle of space, you can win a game by taking so much space away from your opponent that all he can do is pace back and forth in his little cell, waiting for you to proceed with the execution.

The Space Count System

The space count system enables you to count the squares your pieces and pawns control to determine whether you or your opponent controls more territory. At the beginning of a game, the board is more or less divided in half (see Diagram 71 on the next page). White is said to own the squares in the a1-a4-h4-h1 rectangle. Black owns everything in the a8-a5-h5-h8 rectangle. The space count system kicks in when one of you goes beyond these "personal" squares and starts to take control of territory in the enemy's domain.

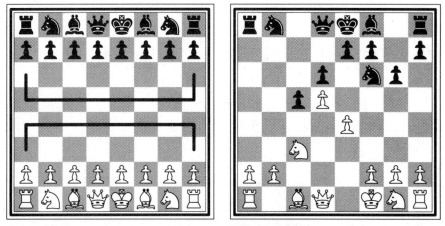

DIAGRAM 71.

DIAGRAM 72.

Let's look at an example from the game between Yasser Seirawan and Bruno Belloti, played in Lugano in 1988. In Diagram 72, who controls more space? Let's count the squares to find out. White's Bishop breaks into Black's territory on g5 and h6: two squares. His Knight on c3 attacks squares b5 and d5: two more squares for a total space count of 4 so far. (Squares e4 and a4 don't count, because they are already considered part of White's territory. We are interested only in squares beyond the 4th rank). The White Queen hits d5 and h5: two more squares, which brings the total space count to 6. That's it for White's pieces.

Now we look at the White pawns. The pawn on d5 controls c6 and e6. The total is now 8. (Remember, a man does not control the square it sits on, so this pawn does not control d5.) The only other man that stabs into Black's territory is the pawn on e4, which controls d5 and f5. Adding 2 to 8 gives us a total space count of 10.

Next, we'll count Black's squares. His Rook on a8 hits a big three enemy squares: a4, a3, and a2. His Knight on f6 hits two: e4 and g4. So far we have a total space count of 5. No other Black pieces can lash out at squares in White's territory, so let's turn our attention to his pawns. The only pawn that can stake a claim in White's space is the pawn on c5, which controls b4 and d4. Black's total is 7. Therefore, White has a space count advantage of 3.

Of course, space is just one of the factors to be considered when evaluating this position. Other factors are

■ White's King has moved and is thus unable to castle.

■ White is a pawn (1 point) ahead.

■ Black has one pawn island, whereas White has two. (Pawn islands are described in Chapter Five, "The Fourth Principle: Pawn Structure.")

■ After Black castles and moves his Rook to the b-file, both of his Rooks will sit on half-open files and be able to attack the White pawns on a2 and b2. Neither of White's Rooks will sit on equivalently active files.

In this game, both sides had factors working in their favor. Because of White's space advantage, I was glad to be playing White from this position.

QUIZ 22. In Diagram 73, who is ahead in the space count? What is the count for each side?

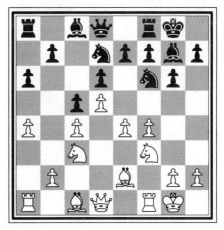

DIAGRAM 73.

The Invincible Capablanca

Though most people love to look at the games of the great attacking masters, some of the most successful players in history have been the quiet positional players. These players slowly grind you down by taking away your space, tying up your pieces, and leaving you with virtually nothing to do! Of all the great positional players, probably the most feared was the Cuban genius José Raúl Capablanca (1888–1942), a man considered in his prime to be virtually unbeatable. Possessing a simple and clear style, Capablanca was particularly famous for his endgame skill. During the first two phases of a game, he was content to gain some advantage in space, convert it into a small material edge (one pawn ahead), and then trade pieces. In the endgame, he would convert his extra pawn into a Queen and win the game easily.

After winning the World Championship from Emanuel Lasker in 1921, Capablanca lost his title to Alexander Alekhine in 1927 because of overconfidence. He really thought nobody could beat him, so he failed to prepare properly for the contest. Though Capablanca continued to play in tournaments in the hopes of getting another shot at Alekhine, the new World Champion made a point of never allowing him a return match. Capablanca's final chess event was the Chess Olympiad of 1939, where he played first board for the Cuban team. Three years later, he died of a stroke in New York.

José Capablanca, chess genius.

How to Use a Space Advantage

A space advantage makes your pieces more mobile than your opponent's. Let's see how Rooks, Bishops, and Knights can make use of extra space.

Rooks and Open Files

To make maximum use of your Rooks, you must understand the following principle:

Rooks need open files to be effective.

A Rook reaches its full potential (in terms of square control) only on open files or ranks. Because the Rook is hemmed in at the start of the game, your task is usually to maneuver it to an open file.

Here is an example from the game between José Capablanca and Karel Treybal, which was played in Carlsbad in 1929. In Diagram 74, White has an enormous advantage in space. He increases this advantage with his next move:

1.   b6

Now Black is forced back even further. Notice how he can move only on the 7th and 8th ranks, whereas White has the first six ranks as his stomping ground. If you do a space count for this position, you'll find that the count for White is

DIAGRAM 74.

- Knight: 2 (e5 and g5).

- Bishop: 3 (f5, b5, and a6).

- Queen: 5 (c5, a5, a6, a7, and a8).

- Rook on h2: 2 (h5 and h6).

- Pawns: 11.

The total is 23!

The space count for Black is considerably less:

- ■ Queen: 1 (f4).
- ■ Pawns: 4.

Just 5 in all.

The Black Queen is under attack, so Black plays

| 1. | ... | Qb8 |
| 2. | Ra1 | |

Though White's advantage in territory is huge, he still has the problem of how to break through. The first thing White does is place his Rooks on the only open file (a1-a8) to prevent the Black Rooks from taking over the a-file. After White has control of the a-file, he can make a decisive penetration from there.

| 2. | ... | Rc8 |

Black is so squeezed that there is nothing for him to do. White can take all the time he wants, without fear of a Black counterattack.

| 3. | Qb4 | |

With this move, Capablanca demonstrates another principle:

When placing your Rooks and Queen on an open file, try to lead with the Rooks to ensure the safety of the Queen.

As in the opening, the Queen should follow the rest of its army. With this in mind, the point of White's move becomes clearer: The Queen steps out of the way to allow the Rooks to penetrate into Black's territory.

| 3. | ... | Rhd8 |
| 4. | Ra7 | |

The Rook is in! White noticed that the weak link in Black's position is the pawn on b7, which is not guarded by another pawn. White will therefore start to bring as much of his army as possible to bear on this pawn.

| 4. | ... | Kf8 |

Poor Black can only go back and forth, hoping that White won't find a way to lower the boom on his position.

5.	Rh1	

Reinforcements! This Rook will join its twin on the open a-file.

5.	...	Be8	7.	R1a4	Kf8
6.	Rha1	Kg8	8.	Qa3	

As shown in Diagram 75, White has completed his domination of the open file. The difference between the range of possible activity for White's Queen and Rooks and the range for Black's is very apparent.

The rest of this game is not related to the topic of how to make maximum use of Rooks, but I will include it anyway, as an illustration of Capablanca's style. The game also serves to point out some of the problems of a space disadvantage.

DIAGRAM 75.

8.	...	Kg8
9.	Kg3	

Secure in the knowledge that Black can do nothing, White treads water to lull the opponent into a sense of security.

9.	...	Bd7	12.	Kg3	Kf8
10.	Kh4	Kh8	13.	Kg2	Be8
11.	Qa1	Kg8	14.	Nd2	

Finally, White moves into action! Remember, White's target is the pawn on b7. To increase the pressure, he brings his Knight to a5, from where the Knight will work with the a7-Rook to try to devour the pawn.

| 14. | ... | Bd7 | 16. | Na5 | Nd8 |
| 15. | Nb3 | Re8 | | | |

Just in time, Black manages to defend the pawn. Can White attack it with anything else?

17. Ba6!!

Most effective! In Diagram 76, you can see that White is attacking the b7-pawn again and now threatens simply to win it by Bxb7. But wait a

minute! Isn't White's Bishop on a6 vulnerable to the b7-pawn?

17. ... bxa6

Black has a temporary advantage in force. White counters with

18. Rxd7

White has recovered material and threatens to capture a pawn with Rxh7. If Black guards against the threat with 18...Kg8, then 19.Nb3 would open up a battery on the a-file against the weak pawn on a6, which

DIAGRAM 76.

would prove undefendable. If White eats this pawn, his material advantage should decide the game. So Black decides to play

18. ... Re7

This allows a snappy finish.

19. Rxd8+!

The simpler 19.Rxe7 Kxe7 20.Nb3 would have captured the a6-pawn and thus would have been good enough for an eventual win. However, the move played is even better. White is setting himself up to use the Knight fork, which I described in Chapter Two, "The First Principle: Force."

19.	...	Rxd8
20.	Nxc6	

White takes a pawn and threatens both of Black's Rooks and his Queen simultaneously! Black gives up here, because 20...Qc8 21.Nxe7 Kxe7 22.Rxa6 would leave White with a two-pawn advantage and an easy win. From 22.Rxa6, play might have continued 22...Rd7 23.Ra7 Rxa7 24.Qxa7+ Qd7 25.c6 Qxa7 26.bxa7, followed by 27.a8=Q. Then the extra Queen would have led to a quick checkmate.

Congratulations! Perhaps without even realizing it, you have just played the game of a World Champion. You will find that playing over the games of great players (which are documented in countless books) is both instructive and fun. Not only will you come to appreciate the artistry of chess, but you will gain insight into how the Grandmasters win their games, and in time, you can hope to emulate their methods.

Bishops and Open Diagonals

Like Rooks, Bishops don't like to be hemmed in by pawns. They need open diagonals if they are to reach their full potential. Bearing the needs of your Bishops in mind, you should try to place your pawns and your Bishops on squares of opposite colors.

In Diagram 77, it is White's turn to play. White has three significant advantages:

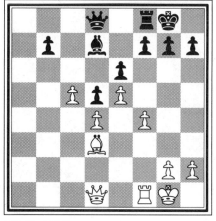

DIAGRAM 77.

■ He has a large advantage in space. (The space count is 14 to 4 in White's favor.)

■ Black has a weak pawn on b7. A pawn is considered weak
if it lies on an open file and cannot be defended by another
pawn. I will go into more detail about pawn strengths and
weaknesses in Chapter Five, "The Fourth Principle: Pawn
Structure."

■ The White Bishop is much more active than its counterpart on d7. White's Bishop, free of all obstructions, is
known as a "good Bishop." Black's pathetic creature on
d7, blocked by its own pawns, is known as a "bad Bishop."

Because it is White's turn to move, he can use a tactic called the
double attack—a maneuver in which one player attacks two points in
the enemy's position simultaneously. Can you find White's move?

The answer is 1.Qb1!, by which the Queen and Bishop bear down on
the pawn on h7 and the Queen attacks the pawn on b7. Black has no way
to defend both pawns, so he must allow White to capture one of them.

The Fianchettoed Bishop: One way to place a Bishop on the longest
possible diagonal is to fianchetto it. A White Bishop is said to be

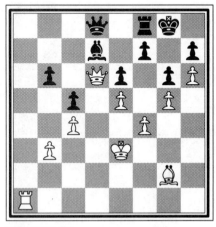

DIAGRAM 78.

fianchettoed if it is placed on g2 or
b2. A Black Bishop is fianchettoed
if it is placed on g7 or b7.

In Diagram 78, the White
fianchettoed Bishop on g2 is clearly
superior to the Black Bishop on d7.
With his Bishop searing down the
h1-a8 diagonal, White threatens to
penetrate Black's position with
Ra8. Another threat is 1.Rd1, by
which White pins the Black Bishop

on d7 and wins it. In the diagram, it is Black's move, but the following factors make his life difficult:

- His lack of space—the space count is 28 to 3 against him.
- His inferior Bishop.
- The White Rook's control of an open file, by means of which White threatens to penetrate Black's position.

Black's best move appears to be

| 1. | ... | **Bc8** |

This play puts the Bishop on a safer square and stops any pins on the d-file. However, after

| 2. | **Qxd8** | **Rxd8** |
| 3. | **Ra8** | |

White creates a winning pin on the 8th rank. Giving in to the inevitable, Black plays

| 3. | ... | **Kf8** |

If Black instead protects his Rook with 3...Rf8, White would create a zugzwang position with 4.Bc6!. (*Zugzwang* is a German word for a situation in which one would like to do nothing. However, the rules of the game state that you must make a move when it is your turn.) Black would be forced to play, even though anything he does will actually hurt his position. After 3...Rf8 4.Bc6, Black would have to give up material. Let's pause to examine all his possible replies:

- 4...Kh8 5.Bb7 Bxb7 6.Rxf8 checkmate.
- 4...Rd8, which transposes into the game, returning to the main line.
- 4...Re8 5.Bxe8.
- 4...Bb7 5.Rxf8+ Kxf8 6.Bxb7, which puts White a Bishop ahead.

- 4...Bd7 5.Rxf8+ and 6.Bxd7.

- 4...Ba6 5.Rxa6.

- 4...b5 5.cxb5, which leaves Black with the same problems
  as before.

- 4...f6 5.exf6 (5.gxf6 is also good) 5...Kf7 6.Ke4! Rd8 7.Ke5
  Rf8 8.Kd6 Rd8+ 9.Kc7. The Bishop on c8 is a goner.

The last option is a good illustration of the power of a King in an endgame. After enough pieces have been traded, the King becomes quite a strong piece!

After this interesting diversion, let's go back to the position that existed after 3...Kf8 (which you can see in Diagram 79).

    4.   Bb7!

White pins the Black Bishop. If Black does nothing to unpin his poor Bishop, White will simply take it and be ahead by 3 points.

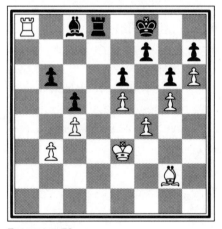

DIAGRAM 79.

    4.   ...   Bxb7

    5.   Rxd8+

Now White is ahead by 2 points (Bishop = 3 points, Rook = 5). The Rook's power is clearly shown after the following moves:

    5.   ...   Ke7

    6.   Rh8

This is a greedy Rook!

6.	...	Bc6	9.	h7	Bd7
7.	Rxh7	Kf8	10.	Rb8	
8.	Rh8+	Ke7			

followed by

11. h8=Q

for an easy win.

The Knight as Advance Scout

Knights are not long-range pieces like Bishops and Rooks, as illustrated in Diagram 80. Here, both minor pieces are in a corner. (Remember, Bishops and Knights are called minor pieces, whereas Rooks and Queens are called major pieces.) From its corner position on a1, the Bishop controls a hefty seven squares. The poor Knight on h1 cannot compete in terms of space count: It controls only two squares.

Does that mean Bishops are better than Knights? No, it just means that you must move your Knight to an advanced square if you want it to reach its potential. To demonstrate, let's relocate that unfortunate Knight from h1 to the e5 central square. Now the Knight controls eight squares, four of which are in the enemy camp and therefore qualify as space-count squares. If the Knight penetrates deeper into Black's territory (say, to e6), the Knight still controls only eight squares, but six of them are now in the enemy camp.

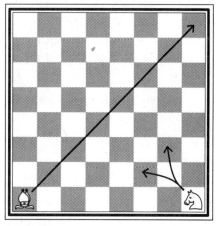

DIAGRAM 80.

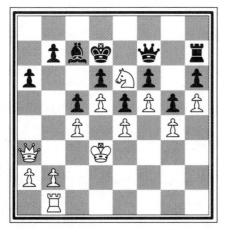

DIAGRAM 81.

Bearing these strengths and weaknesses in mind, our battle cry for Knights should be "Forward! Ever forward!" Because of the Knight's unique ability to jump over other pieces, it does not need to open up the battle lines to strut its stuff. Give your Knights an assignment in an advanced outpost and they will wreak havoc on the enemy at every opportunity.

Here is an example. What is the space count in Diagram 81? When you figure it out, you realize that Black's position is very bad. The lopsided space count (a crushing 20 to 6) leaves Black with very little room. In particular, note the difference between the Knight and Bishop. The White Knight is firmly entrenched on e6 and is single-handedly eating into Black's position. Black's "bad Bishop" is hopelessly blocked by its own pawns and reduced to inactivity.

To win this game, White needs only to penetrate through Black's wall of pawns with his Rook and Queen. How can he do this? Refer to the discussion of Rooks earlier in this chapter, where I stressed the importance of giving your Rooks open files. Remember, you should always try to increase the activity of your pieces!

In Diagram 81, it is White's turn to play. From this position the best move is

1.   b4!

Shame on you if you wanted to play 1.Nxc7, because after 1...Kxc7, you would have managed to trade your wonderful Knight for Black's wretched Bishop. Notice that the point count—the measure of force—would have remained even after such a trade.

The superior 1.b4 immediately gives the White Rook more scope and also threatens to capture the pawn on c5 with 2.bxc5. If Black defends his c5-pawn with 1...b6, the pawn on a6 becomes vulnerable to capture by the White Queen, with 2.Qxa6. Black instead answers with

    1.   ...   cxb4

to which White replies

    2.   Qxb4

Now the White Queen, backed up by the Rook on b1, attacks the b7-pawn. Because 2...Kc8 would lose horribly to 3.Qxb7+ Kd7 4.Qxc7+ Ke8 5.Qd8 checkmate, Black must advance his b7-pawn and hope for the best:

    2.   ...   b6

Now White can maneuver to capture the pawn on a6 or, if he wishes, the pawn on b6. In Diagram 82, can you see how he would win these pawns?

To win the a6-pawn, White uses the fork tactic, discussed in Chapter Two, "The First Principle: Force." The fork is accomplished by

    3.   Qa4+

which mounts a simultaneous attack on both the Black King on d7 and the pawn on a6. Black then plays

    3.   ...   Kc8

because 3...Ke7 would lose the Black Bishop, which has nothing guarding it, to 4.Nxc7.

    4.   Qxa6+ Kd7

If Black plays 4...Kb8 instead, White would be able to win in several ways. One method would be 5.Rb3 Qd7 6.Ra3, followed by Qa8 checkmate. As it is, White plays

    5.   Qb7

DIAGRAM 82.

The White Queen and the Knight can now launch a combined attack on the Bishop on c7.

    5.   **...**   **Ke8**

Black would prefer to move his King to d8, but the impudent White Knight won't allow him to.

    6.   **Qc8+** **Ke7**

    7.   **Qxc7+** **Ke8**

Black would like to run away with 7...Kf8, but the White Knight controls square f8, too!

    8.   **Qd8 checkmate**

Now look back at Diagram 82. You can see that 3.Qa4+ is a very strong move. However, I did say that White has the option of capturing the b6-pawn instead of the a6-pawn. To make this capture, White plays

    3.   **Nxc7**

White does not relish the idea of trading his wonderful Knight, but this move is a good demonstration of a basic principle:

Destroy the defender and the target will fall!

In this case, destroying the Black Bishop leads to the capture of the b6-pawn. As well as capturing a pawn (1 point), White is also enabling his Rook and Queen to decisively penetrate Black's position. Black has no choice but to play

    3.   **...**   **Kxc7**

or White would simply go back to e6 and be 3 points ahead.

    4.   **Qxb6+** **Kd7**

    5.   **Qa7+**

The White Queen steps away from the b-file to allow the Rook to charge forward.

    5.   **...**   **Ke8**

    6.   **Rb8 checkmate**

QUIZ 23. Placing your pawns on the same color squares as your Bishop is:

- A good idea, because all your pawns can be defended by the Bishop.

- A bad idea, because the pawns block the Bishop and therefore reduce its potential sphere of activity.

As it turned out, capturing either the a6-pawn or the b6-pawn led to a win. But because you have to work so hard to get your Knights into enemy territory, think twice before trading them.

Memorization versus Understanding

I was just 13, and my opponent, also a young boy, was making his first moves very quickly. It was obvious that he had memorized this particular opening and was repeating the moves of some famous Grandmaster. Cautiously, I picked my way through his opening "minefield" and was only slightly behind when the middlegame started. He finally began to slow down, taking more time to think over his moves. "At least we're out of the book now, and he's on his own," I thought with a good deal of relief. The battle was joined and I needed to concentrate.

Ten moves later my opponent resigned. It became obvious that he had a good memory but understood little about the principles of chess. Left to his own devices, his game fell apart remarkably quickly.

I have played this type of game repeatedly throughout my career. So many players start out by thinking that memorization is the key to success. Take my word for it: A good memory is useful, but without a firm knowledge of chess fundamentals, you are doomed to constant defeat.

How to Gain a Space Advantage in the Opening

Rather than waste your time memorizing openings, you will do better to keep yourself fresh and play every opening move with particular goals in mind. With every turn you must ask yourself whether you are

- Acquiring superior force in some part of the board.

- Gaining a lead in development.

- Improving your pawn structure (discussed in Chapter Five, "The Fourth Principle: Pawn Structure").

- Gaining space.

Let's see how these questions help in actual opening play. In the commentary, I am speaking from White's viewpoint.

1.   e4

This move gives me a space count of 5 (the f1-Bishop controls b5 and a6, the Queen controls h5, and the pawn controls d5 and f5) and frees two of my pieces. I could gain an advantage in development if my opponent is not careful.

1.   ...   Nf6

He is attacking my e4-pawn! That's a frisky move for Black to play. I could just defend my pawn with 2.Nc3, but after 2...e5 I would not have made any significant gain in time. I'll try to punish him for bringing his Knight ahead of his pawns.

2.   e5

By attacking his Knight, I force him to move it again, so we will both have moved the same piece twice. However, I'm hoping that his Knight will be more vulnerable in the middle of the board. It's interesting that I am still racking up only 2 points of space count with this pawn. No matter how deeply a pawn goes into an opponent's position, it can never control more than two squares.

    2.   ...   Ne4?

What on earth is he doing with his Knight? Surely he doesn't expect to beat me with this lone piece. I'll attack the Knight again. Either he will have to let me take it, which will give me an advantage in material, or he will have to keep moving it, which will give me an advantage in both time and space.

    3.   d3

With one move, I attack his Knight and free my Bishop on c1. I learned long ago that moves like 3.Bd3 are bad, because they block my own d2-pawn, which in turn blocks my c1-Bishop. I certainly don't want to entomb my own pieces!

    3.   ...   Nc5

No choice. He can't go to d6 or f6 because of my pawn; g5 is covered by my c1-Bishop. I suspect that Black is not familiar with the concept of time. Moving his Knight again and again is clearly in violation of this principle.

    4.   d4

I've moved this pawn twice, but the play is justified because it forces him to move his Knight yet again. Anyway, the pawn on d3 was blocking my Bishop on f1.

    4.   ...   Na6

    5.   Nf3

Let's sum up this position. Black has moved his Knight four times. I have managed to advance both of my center pawns. As a result, I now have a significant advantage both in development and in space (the space count is 10 to 1).

    This brief demonstration shows the importance of bringing out your pieces and pawns quickly. They help you fight for the territory you need to move about freely.

DIAGRAM 83.

The Role of Defender

Make no mistake about it: Everyone likes to attack. However, even the best players sometimes find themselves in an inferior position that requires hours of calm, defensive play. In the top levels of modern chess, every Grandmaster knows how to attack and defend with equal skill. That was not always the case. In the early 1800s, players virtually lived for attack. They would happily sacrifice everything for the chance of a nice checkmate. Though they often succeeded, success was due more to the lackluster defensive play of the time than it was to their attacking skills. For example, an unspoken rule stated that if your opponent sacrificed a piece, you were duty-bound to capture it, even if the capture signalled your own bloody doom.

This lemming-like obedience came to an end with the rise of the first official World Champion, Wilhelm Steinitz (1836–1900). In the *British Chess Magazine* of January 1892, James Cunningham described Steinitz as follows: "He is a man of great physical vigour, and possesses a well-preserved constitution. Everything about him denotes power rather than grace, strength rather than beauty. His features are rugged in outline and his face is the face of a man of action rather than a man of thought."

Steinitz started out playing in the berserker style of the day, but he eventually came up with several new and profound positional ideas, which led him to drastically alter his style and become the first true positional player. He would start out with a somewhat passive game

Wilhelm Steinitz, the first great defender.

and would not worry about being attacked as long as he had certain positional trumps. (He particularly favored a superior pawn structure.)

After more than 20 years of dominating world chess, Steinitz was finally beaten by the great Emanuel Lasker. He lost his title and then lost the rematch. In failing health and severe poverty (in those days, it was very difficult for a chess professional to make a living), Steinitz came unglued mentally. He died a pauper in New York.

How to Defend Against a Space Advantage

Sooner or later, you will find yourself squeezed by your opponent into a cramped position, so you need to know how to defend against such a tactic. Remember the following principle:

The player with less space should try to trade some pieces.

You may find it helpful to think of a cramped position as being like overpopulation. Twenty people in a small house are crowded and very uncomfortable. Two people in the same house have all the space they need. Let's look at an example of this principle translated into strategy:

1. d4 d5
2. c4

A good move. White puts pressure on the d5-pawn and makes preparations for the eventual opening of the c-file for his Rooks with cxd5. Though this opening is called the Queen's Gambit, no gambit is really involved. If Black captures the c4-pawn with 2...dxc4, White can even the score in several ways, the quickest being 3.Qa4+ followed by Qxc4. After White captures the pawn, he would follow up with e2-e4 to acquire a full pawn center. Because of that possibility, Black's usual response to the Queen's Gambit is to decline the capture on c4 and instead guard his d5-pawn:

2. ... e6

This is the most common move, though 2...c6 is also good. Not so good is 2...Nf6, because after 3.cxd5 Nxd5 4.e4, White would once again acquire a full pawn center and all the space that comes with it.

3. Nc3

White continues to develop pieces and put pressure on the d5-pawn. Notice how the Knight fits comfortably behind the c4-pawn; the two work together to attack Black's center.

3. ... Nf6

A sensible reply. Black also develops his pieces, at the same time giving additional support to the d5-pawn.

4. Bg5

White pins the Black Knight, one of the defenders of the d5-pawn. Notice how White is quickly developing his pieces and at the same time using three of his men to directly or indirectly put pressure on square d5.

Here's another important point: White would like to play e3 and free his f1-Bishop. However, if he makes this move too early, he will block the c1-Bishop. By moving the c1-Bishop first, White will be free to follow up with e3. Remember, whenever possible avoid blocking your pieces with your pawns.

Black's next move is to break the pin on his Knight:

| 4. | ... | Be7 |

Now, if the Knight moves, the Bishop on g5 will not attack the Queen. Black has developed a new piece and is preparing to castle.

| 5. | e3 |

White frees the f1-Bishop and gives more support to his pawn on d4.

| 5. | ... | O-O |
| 6. | Nf3 |

White has developed his unmoved Knight.

| 6. | ... | Nbd7 |

Black also moves his other Knight into the battle. He avoids 6...Nc6, because he sees that he will have to use his c-pawn to give added defense to the d5-pawn. A 6...Nc6 move would block the pawn and make it unusable.

| 7. | Rc1 |

White is anticipating the eventual removal of his pawn on c4 (either because White will play cxd5 or because Black will take it with ...dxc4), so he places his Rook on the soon-to-be-opened c-file.

| 7. | ... | c6 |

Black gives more support to the d5-pawn and also gives the Queen a little room to move.

| 8. | Bd3 |

DIAGRAM 84.

White develops the Bishop and prepares to castle. So far both sides have played sensibly. It's now time to take stock. What is going on in the position in Diagram 84?

First, do a space count. You should come up with 13 to 6. In case your space count is different, let's run quickly through it so that you can see where you went wrong. Start with White. White's pawns on d4 and c4 control four squares (e5, d5, c5, and b5). His Knights control another four (g5, e5, d5, and b5). His g5-Bishop controls two (f6 and h6) and his d3-Bishop controls three (f5, g6, and h7). These numbers add up to a total space count of 13. Now for Black. Only his d5-pawn strikes into enemy territory, so we count 2 for his pawns. His f6-Knight controls two squares (e4 and g4). Finally, his e7-Bishop controls another two squares (b4 and a3). The squares add up to a total space count of 6 for Black.

With this space count, we have confirmed that White has more territory than Black. Because of Black's lack of breathing room, Black is unable to move his Rooks to useful files, and his Bishop on c8 is completely blocked. Obviously, Black must do something about this undesirable state of affairs.

Fortunately for Black, Capablanca gave this position some attention many years ago and came up with a solution. His reasoning went something like this: Because Black's position is cramped, he must initiate a series of trades to give himself more room to move. Then Black must stake a bigger claim in the center and advance either his c6- or e6-pawn, challenging White's central position and striking out for still more space.

■■■■■■■■■■■■■■■■■■■■■■■■■■■■■■■■■■■■■

QUIZ 25. You have a large space advantage and your opponent attempts to trade some pieces. What should you do?

■ Let him trade; trades can only work in your favor.

■ Avoid trades as much as possible.

■ Invoke the en passant rule.

Black has no choice but to try this tactic:

8. ... dxc4!

The first trade.

9. Bxc4 Nd5!

More trades. White's g5-Bishop cannot avoid being traded.

10. Bxe7 Qxe7

You can see that Black already has extra elbow room.

11. O-O

White avoids 11.Bxd5 or 11.Nxd5 because then 11...exd5! would give Black just what he wants: The Bishop on c8 would no longer be blocked by a pawn.

11. ... Nxc3!

One more trade. Black wanted to play ...e6-e5, but if he made this move too early, he would lose a pawn; for example, 11...e5? 12.Nxd5 cxd5 13.Bxd5. Then the Knight on d5 would have more attackers than defenders.

12. Rxc3 e5

Having given himself more room, Black solves his one remaining problem: the blocked Bishop on c8. By pushing the e5-pawn, Black has freed his Bishop and expanded its territory.

13. dxe5 Nxe5

14. Nxe5 Qxe5

Now that Black has traded pieces and freed his Bishop, he obviously has plenty of room to move about in. Let's do another space count to confirm the wisdom of this strategy: 10 to 9. Black's space count is now almost equal to White's! Play over this example several times, trying to get a feel for the space-giving powers of a trade.

Tests

TEST 17. What is the space count?

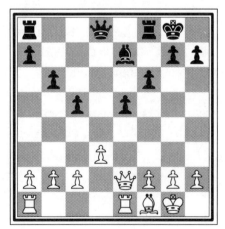

TEST 18. It is White's turn to play. Both Bishops seem blocked by their pawns. What should White do in this situation?

TEST 19. It is Black's turn to play. Do a space count. Because White controls more territory, would 1...Be6 be a sensible move?

The Fourth Principle: Pawn Structure

C learly the weakest man on the board, the little pawn may seem unimportant. In reality, though, the pawn is the foundation upon which most chess strategies are built. The great Polish Grandmaster Saviely Tartakower (1887–1956) was not joking when he wrote, "Never lose a pawn and you will never lose a game."

The Importance of Pawns

In the 17th and 18th centuries, the power of pawns was universally underrated. It took the legendary French player François-André Philidor (1726–95) to demonstrate that correct handling of the pawns could make a major difference in a game. In 1749, he published a chess book that gave detailed instructions on how to play the middlegame. His comment "Les pions sont l'âme du jeu" (Pawns are the soul of the game) became one of the most famous chess sayings.

Philidor quite rightly believed that ignorance of the correct way to handle pawns was the primary weakness of his chess-playing contemporaries. But, like most people who are ahead of their time, he was misunderstood. Some players thought he was claiming that the ability to promote a pawn to a Queen made pawns stronger than pieces. Other players did not know what to make of his theories. Though worshiped in chess circles, Philidor was never really appreciated in his lifetime for his

André Philidor: "Pawns are the soul of chess."

great insights. That level of appreciation came only many years after his death.

Less than one hundred years later, in 1857, Paul Morphy dominated the chess world. Able to calculate with immense speed and precision and possessing wonderful technique, Morphy played a wide-open, attacking game that made little use of pawns. Those were the days of never-ending attacks and blood-soaked boards, and even Morphy could not properly handle closed positions in which pawn play was the critical factor. Philidor was still not fully understood.

After Morphy retired, Wilhelm Steinitz gradually assumed the mantle of chess leader. In 1873, he changed his style and, with single-minded determination, succeeded in also changing the style of world chess. Positional and defensive ideas became prominent. The intricacies of pawn formations and pawn weaknesses became hot topics of discussion. By 1905, Philidor had been completely vindicated. Now, in the 1990s, his ideas have become common property and are passed along to all players, just as I will now pass them on to you.

When You Leave Pawns at Home

In the game-opening examples I've shown you, the players have moved both their pieces and their pawns. Some beginners think they should leave their pawns at home, moving them only when necessary to make way for their pieces. Let's see what happens when such a player (White) meets an opponent (Black) who uses his pawns to control space in the center of the board.

    1.   Nc3

White immediately gets a piece out. Remember, White's strategy is to move as few pawns as possible.

    1. ...   d5

Black takes control of some of the central squares. So far the space count is even: 2 to 2.

    2.   Nf3   c5

Black uses his pawns to restrict the movements of White's pieces. Note how the d5-pawn takes control of square e4 away from the c3-Knight, and the c5-pawn takes control of square d4 away from the f3-Knight.

    3.   d3

Finally, White must move a pawn to get a Bishop out.

    3. ...   Nc6

This Knight fits very nicely behind the c5-pawn. Pawn and Knight can now work together to put pressure on square d4. So far, Black has built up a space-count edge of 8 to 6.

    4.   Bg5?

White pins Black's e7-pawn. However, White's pieces will now be chased back by the Black pawns.

    4. ...   f6   **6.   Bg3   Be6**

    5.   Bf4   e5

White's pieces are hemmed in because Black's pawns control the center.

As Diagram 85 on the following page shows, the space count stands at 5 for White to 10 for Black. White's pawnless strategy has clearly been unsuccessful. Moreover, the example demonstrates that moving one or two pawns does not lose time, because the opponent must also move his pawns. If he doesn't, his prematurely advanced pieces will be chased backward, resulting in a gain of time for the opponent's pawns.

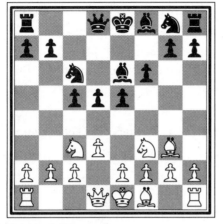

DIAGRAM 85.

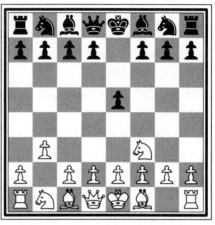

DIAGRAM 86.

Why did White's strategy fail? The answer hinges on the fact that pawns are worth less than pieces. When a pawn attacks a Bishop, Knight, or Rook, the more powerful piece feels compelled to retreat. When David meets Goliath in chess, the giant gets out of the way! Thus, it makes good sense to lead off a game with your pawns. They clear the road for the heavy artillery.

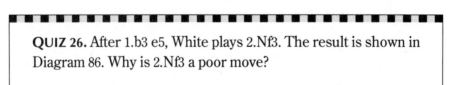

QUIZ 26. After 1.b3 e5, White plays 2.Nf3. The result is shown in Diagram 86. Why is 2.Nf3 a poor move?

What Is Pawn Structure?

The health and the positioning of all the pawns is called *pawn structure*. (It is also called *pawn formation*, or *pawn skeleton*.) If White has many weak pawns whereas Black's pawns are all well defended, Black is said to have a superior pawn structure.

118

Many players fail to appreciate that the positioning of the pawns dictates the strategies available to both sides. For example, if one side has advanced his pawns and thus gained a space advantage, the other side's strategy might be to trade pieces and decrease crowding in his cramped quarters. If one side's pawn formation is full of weak pawns, the other side's strategy might be to attack these weak men.

What Makes a Pawn Weak?

When a boxer notices that he has cut his opponent, he repeatedly jabs at the cut in the hopes of making it bad enough for the ring doctor to stop the fight. The same logic applies in chess. If your opponent has a weak pawn (a wound), focus your army on that pawn and make every effort to capture it. Let's take a look at the most typical types of weak pawns: pawn islands and doubled, tripled, isolated, and backward pawns.

Pawn Islands

It stands to reason that as you move your pawns, they break rank. With every pawn move, what was a solid rank of pawns becomes more and more fragmented. Single pawns or groups of pawns that are separated from other pawns by at least one file are called *pawn islands*. Diagram 87 shows three pawn islands for White (a2-b2, d4, and f2-g2-h2) and two for Black (a7-b6 and e6-f7-g7-h7). Remember Capablanca's warning: "In the endgame, whoever has the most pawn islands loses."

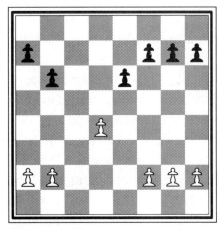

DIAGRAM 87.

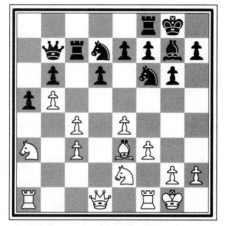

DIAGRAM 88.

Doubled Pawns

A pawn that makes a capture and ends up on the same file but in front of another pawn of the same color is said to be doubled. Doubled pawns are usually considered weak, because they do not have the mobility of normal pawns. On occasion, though, a doubled pawn on a center file can be useful, because the pawn can control central squares that normal pawns cannot.

In Diagram 88, White's pawns on c4 and c3 are doubled. The pawn on c4 is the one in trouble, because it is unfortunately sitting on a half-open file and vulnerable to attack by several of Black's pieces. If White's c3-pawn was sitting on d3, his c4-pawn would be solidly protected by another pawn and would be quite safe. As it is, Black can launch an all-out attack on the weakling on c4.

    1.   **...**   **Ne5**

Black attacks the c4-pawn with both his Knight and his c7-Rook and threatens to capture the pawn with 2...Nxc4. White defends the pawn with

    2.   **Qa4**

White has fended off the double attack. Is the pawn safe? No. One more attacker should be enough to break the defender's back.

    2.   **...**   **Rfc8**

Now the pawn is attacked three times and White is unable to defend it again. After a move like 3.Rfd1, Black would play 3...Nxc4. After 4.Nxc4 Rxc4, Black would start to work on the c3-pawn.

This example shows that if an advanced pawn is not defended by another pawn, it can become weak. Doubled pawns are not a liability as

long as the front one is defended by a pawn, as you can see from the
following opening sequence:

1.	e4	e5	4.	d3	d6
2.	Nf3	Nc6	5.	O-O	Nf6
3.	Bc4	Bc5	6.	Be3!	

Has White gone mad? He is voluntarily creating a situation in which his
pawns will be doubled.

| 6. | ... | Bxe3 |

Black happily obliges.

| 7. | fxe3 |

What has White gained with his doubled pawns? Take a look at Diagram
89. First, White has gained an open file for his f1-Rook. Because Black
does not have an open file for his Rooks, the open file gives White's Rooks
an advantage. Second, White has traded the very active Black Bishop on
c5 for the previously undeveloped White Bishop on c1. Third, and most
important: The combined action of Black's c6-Knight, c5-Bishop, and
e5-pawn brought a good deal of pressure to bear on square d4. At any
moment, Black might have moved a piece to this square (for example, by
playing Nd4). Now White's pawn
on e3 takes control of square d4
away from Black altogether. Finally, White allowed his pawns to
be doubled because the foremost
pawn on e4 is solidly defended by
the pawn on d3. As a result, the
White pawns on e3 and e4 are not
only safe but are highly useful, because they combine to put pressure
on four critical center squares (d4,
f4, d5, and f5).

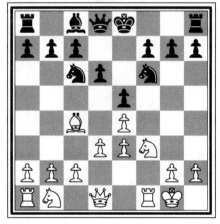

DIAGRAM 89.

Tripled Pawns

Though doubled pawns can be useful, tripled pawns are always an out-and-out liability. They are invariably undefended by other pawns and are usually sitting ducks for an enemy attack. The square directly in front of tripled pawns can easily fall into the clutches of an enemy piece, supplying an excellent outpost because no pawns are around to chase the piece away.

In Diagram 90, White's tripled pawns are undefended by other pawns and are doomed to eventual capture by the enemy. Black, with the half-open c-file for his Rooks and square c5 for his Knight, can use his whole army to attack the tripled pawns via 1...Rfc8, 2...Nd7, and 3...Nb6. White will then be unable to stop Black from winning the c4-pawn with 4...Nxc4. After Black wins this first pawn, he will turn his attention to the next pawn in line: the one on c3. To put it simply:

Don't triple your pawns!

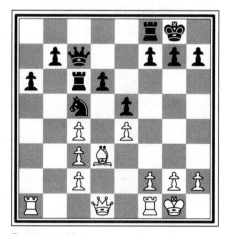

DIAGRAM 90.

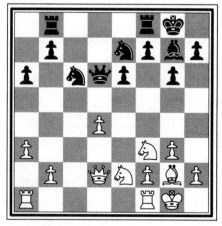

DIAGRAM 91.

Isolated Pawns

An isolated pawn is considered weak because it has no protecting pawns on either side to give it the support it often needs. In Diagram 90, the c4-pawn is isolated as well as tripled. Diagram 91 shows another example of an isolated pawn. Here, the isolated White pawn on d4 cannot be protected by other pawns and must be constantly guarded by pieces. Black can put more and more pressure on the pawn, forcing White to use all his powerful pieces as nursemaids and thereby keeping White in a passive, defensive position. As it turns out, White will lose this pawn anyway, because Black can speedily attack it with everything he's got. Here's how:

| 1. | ... | Nf5 |

Because Black is attacking the pawn with four pieces and White is guarding it with only three, Black simply threatens to take it off the board. White plays

| 2. | Rfd1 |

Making the pawn safe once more. Black brings another attacker into play:

| 2. | ... | Rfd8 |

This time, though, White has run out of defenders, and the pawn will fall.

| 3. | Rac1 | Ncxd4 | 5. | Nxd4 | Bxd4 |
| 4. | Nexd4 | Nxd4 |

Black is now a solid pawn ahead.

Backward Pawns

A backward pawn is one that has fallen behind the other pawns of its own persuasion and can no longer be supported or guarded by them. In

DIAGRAM 92.

DIAGRAM 93.

Diagram 92, on squares d6 and f7 Black has two backward pawns. The pawns on h6 and b7 are not backward because they can safely advance.

QUIZ 27. In Diagram 93, it is Black's turn to play. Point out White's main weakness and identify the best way for Black to attack this weak point.

Safety First

I have introduced you to some players who were vicious attackers and to others who were more positionally inclined. Former World Champion Tigran Petrosyan (1929–84) of the Soviet Union was a different type of player altogether. He was the ultimate "safety first" player. Always careful about his pawn structure, he rarely exposed himself with any kind of pawn weakness. He would go out of his way to stop his opponent's attacks before they even got started.

Criticized for his "boring" playing style, Petrosyan did not win many tournaments, typically taking second or third place. However, he was known as a player who was almost impossible to beat. The critics had to eat their words in 1963,

Tigran Petrosyan, the unbeatable foe.

when he won the World Championship from the great Soviet player Mikhail Botvinnik.

How to Cure a Weak Pawn

A pawn becomes weak when it can no longer be protected by another pawn. Your first defense against weak pawns is to avoid exposing them.

When you advance your pawns, be sure they cannot fall under attack. You can ward off potential attacks by trailing one pawn behind your advanced pawns so that you can bring it forward in case of trouble.

In Diagram 94, the White pawn on e4 is useful because it puts pressure on the important d5 central square and blocks the diagonal of the fianchettoed Bishop on b7.

DIAGRAM 94.

However, Black is starting to mount an attack against this pawn. With the two pieces on b7 and f6 attacking the pawn and only one piece defending it, Black threatens to snap the pawn off the board with ...Nxe4. White could send in another defender with 1.Bf3, but Black would merely increase the pressure with 1...Nc5, and White would then have great difficulty in guarding the pawn. Fortunately, White has foreseen the possibility of this type of attack and has left a trailing pawn to act as guardian if the need arises. By playing 1.f3, White bolsters the pawn's defense and Black has to throw all thoughts of attacking the pawn out the window.

We are all saddled with a weak pawn on occasion. But you can often transform the weakness by either trading the weak pawn or moving it to a square where it is no longer vulnerable.

In Diagram 95, White's pawn on c4 is isolated and weak. Black has taken note and mounted an attack against it. Black hopes to further increase the pressure with ...Rc8, followed by ...Rc7 and ...Qc8. With his mind on what promises to be a very pleasant game, Black has forgotten an important principle:

DIAGRAM 95.

Before you attack a weak pawn, you must gain control of the square directly in front of it.

If you don't control this square, your opponent can advance the pawn. It is White's turn to play, and Black's lapse allows White to take the advantage:

1.   c5!

A very strong move. White makes use of the pin on the d-file (1...dxc5 would merely provoke 2.Rxd8) and turns his "weak" pawn into a battering ram. Now the Black b6-Knight and the a6-Bishop are under attack by the White e2-Bishop.

| 1. | ... | Bxe2 |

Black takes care of the problem of the attacked Bishop. Now White cannot play 2.cxb6 because Black would respond with 2...Bxd1., snaring an *exchange*. (A player wins an exchange when he trades a minor piece for a Rook.)

| 2. | Qxe2 |

White regains material equality and renews the threat against Black's b6-Knight.

| 2. | ... | Nc8 |

| 3. | cxd6 |

Now Black cannot play 3...Nxd6, because 4.e5 would result in a pawn fork against Black's Knights.

| 3. | ... | exd6 |

The situation has undergone a drastic change. White's weak c4-pawn is gone, and Black is left with an isolated pawn on d6. Because White has the square in front of the newly weakened pawn well guarded, he can put pressure on the pawn while simultaneously taking control of more space.

| 4. | Qa6 |

The space count is now a resounding 25 to 2! All of White's pieces are well placed, and both of his Rooks are sitting on beautiful files. Adding White's strengths to Black's weakness on d6, you can see that Black's position is miserable.

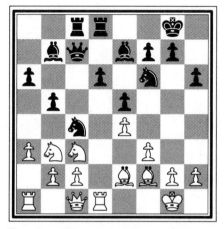

DIAGRAM 96.

Let's look at another example, this time one that favors Black. In Diagram 96, Black has an excellent position. His Rooks are both centrally posted and his c4-Knight is strong (as advanced Knights have a tendency to be).

The one drawback is the backward pawn on d6. Black cures this problem immediately:

1. ... d5!

He gets rid of his one weakness, frees his e7-Bishop, and opens the file for his d8-Rook.

2. exd5 Nxd5

3. Nxd5 Bxd5

With these pieces and a space-count advantage of 11 to 8, Black can be very happy with this position.

QUIZ 28. Which statement is false?

■ Doubled pawns are always weak.

■ Tripled pawns are almost always a problem.

■ If you have a weak pawn, you should either try to trade it or start an attack in another sector of the board so that your opponent does not have time to attack the pawn.

Good Pawns and Pigs on the 7th

A good pawn is any pawn that exerts a cramping pressure on the opponent and is safe from attack. One type of pawn that fits this description is known as a passed pawn, because it has no enemy pawns in front or on either side. Such a pawn is free to advance unless the opponent assigns one of his pieces the passive task of setting up a roadblock in front of it. A passed pawn is useful in the middlegame because it ties up the enemy piece that is blocking its advance, and it is also strong in the endgame because it can run for the border and return as a Queen.

From the position in Diagram 97, White's passed pawn is going to thrash the whole Black army. It is White's turn to play. White would like to promote this pawn to a Queen, but Black has blocked it with his Queen. The way to win such positions is to break the blockade.

1. Qf7

A crushing move, setting up the threat of 2.Qe8+ Qxe8 3.dxe8=Q+, and so on. Black counters with

1. ... Ra8

stopping 2.Qe8+, because 2...Qxe8 3.dxe8=Q+ Rxe8 would then lose the precious White pawn.

2. Re1!

Now White threatens to win everything with 3.Re8+ Qxe8 4.dxe8=Q+ Rxe8 5.Qxe8+. Black is powerless to prevent a major loss of material.

2. ... Qf8

DIAGRAM 97.

129

Also hopeless is 2...Qg8, because it leads to 3.Qf6+ Qg7 4.Re8+ Rxe8 5.dxe8=Q checkmate.

3.	Qxf8+	Rxf8	5.	d8=Q
4.	Re8	Kg7		

Accepting his fate, Black can do nothing better than resign.

This example showed the passed pawn's great desire to metamorphose into a Queen. Aaron Nimzowitsch called this desire the "pawn's lust to expand." In the next example, we'll take a look at another passed pawn, called a protected passed pawn.

The passed pawn on d5 in Diagram 98 is called a protected passed pawn because it is firmly defended by another White pawn. Black must worry about the d5-pawn's advance, but he has no good way of attacking it. Because of the pawn's invulnerability, White is free to leave it on its own and use his pieces elsewhere. In this position, White also controls the only open file and will use it to penetrate Black's position.

    1.   Re7!

The White Rook charges into the heart of Black's territory. Placing a

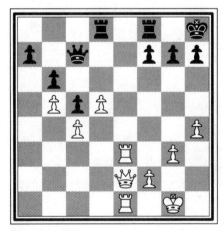

Rook on the 7th rank is considered advantageous, because most of the enemy pawns reside there and thus become vulnerable to attack.

    1.   ...   Rd7

Black offers a trade, hoping to get rid of the e7-Rook.

    2.   Rxd7   Qxd7

    3.   Qe7!

With his protected passed pawn, White will be able to enter any

DIAGRAM 98.

130

endgame with confidence. More importantly, White is still angling for control of the 7th rank.

3. ... Qxe7

An unfortunate necessity. A 3...Rd8 move merely leads to 4.Qxd7 Rxd7 5.Re8 checkmate, which as I've already mentioned is called a Back Rank Mate, and tends to occur frequently.

4. Rxe7

Black loses a pawn because 4...Ra8 (which would guard the a7-pawn) simply exposes the f7-pawn to Rxf7.

As you can see, placing a Rook on the 7th rank is worth some effort. I bring this strategy up in this chapter because a Rook on the 7th is one of the worst enemies a pawn can have! Some players go as far as to say that it's worth losing a pawn to place a Rook on the 7th rank, compensating as it usually does for the temporary 1-point disadvantage.

A Rook on the 7th is nice, but two Rooks doubled on the 7th are more than twice as nice! Take a look at Diagram 99. Here, the material count is even, and it is White's move. White will win by doubling his Rooks on the 7th rank. Rooks in this position are often able to capture everything in their path; their combined might makes them almost unstoppable. In fact, their power to eat everything is so great that two Rooks on the 7th are often called pigs on the 7th. White sets his pigs in motion with

1. Rdd7

Black has no good reply to White's many threats.

1. ... Rf6

DIAGRAM 99.

Moves like 1...h6 would lose to 2.Rxg7+ Kh8 3.Rh7+ Kg8, and then 4.Rdg7 checkmate.

>2.　　Rxg7+　　Kf8
>
>3.　　Rxh7

White threatens 4.Rh8 checkmate.

>3.　　...　　Ke8

White can win in many ways. He could keep feasting with 4.Rxb7 to gain a 3-point material advantage, or he could continue the attack and prepare a pawn for promotion with 4.g5 followed by 5.g6. Play with this position for a while and figure out how you would win the game.

The Pawn Chain

Having dealt with individual pawn weaknesses and the pawn's worst enemy, it's time to discuss pawn chains. A pawn chain is neither bad nor good. It is simply a group of pawns lined up on a diagonal. Each pawn is considered an individual link in the chain.

Pawn chains are created by many kinds of openings. One of the most common pawn chains is an outcome of the French Defense.

1.	e4	e6	4.	e5	Nfd7
2.	d4	d5	5.	f4	c5
3.	Nd2	Nf6	6.	c3	

In the resulting position (see Diagram 100), White has a pawn chain that reaches from b2 to e5. Black's chain reaches from f7 to d5.

The important thing to remember about a pawn chain is that you must attack it at its *base*. The base is the pawn that is not protected by any other pawn—the end of the chain. In Diagram 100, the base of White's pawn chain becomes d4. If Black plays ...cxd4, after White's recapture with cxd4 the d4-pawn will have no pawn defenders. Similarly, the base of Black's pawn chain becomes e6, if White plays f4-f5 and fxe6, after Black's recapture with ...fxe6 the e6-pawn will have no pawn defenders. Let's explore some typical moves from Diagram 100.

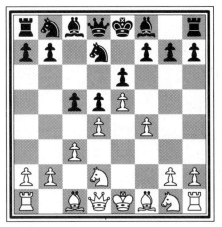

DIAGRAM 100.

6.	...	Nc6

Because Black can at any moment play ...cxd4, creating the d4 base pawn, Black puts more pressure on d4. Remember, as soon as you figure out which pawn is the base or potential base of the chain, rush over and launch an attack!

7.	Ndf3

Why has White moved the same piece twice in the opening? White sees that his one weak point is his d4-pawn. Forewarned is forearmed, so he decides to guard the pawn to the extent possible, to ensure its safety. The more common move 7.Ngf3 would lead to 7...cxd4 8.cxd4 Qb6, by which time the d4-pawn would start to get shaky.

7.	...	Qb6
8.	Ne2	

Now the d4-pawn is well defended and White can implement his plan of playing for an f5 advance and a subsequent attack on Black's pawn on e6.

One other point worth noting about the base attack: When you trade pawns at the base of a pawn chain, you tend to open a file for your Rooks.

133

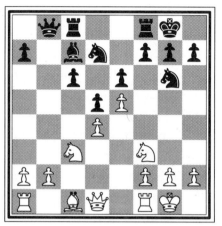

DIAGRAM 101.   **DIAGRAM 102.**

Diagram 101 shows a simplified example. Here, both sides are following their respective plans for a base attack. White hopes to play 1.fxe6 fxe6 2.Bg4 to put pressure on the Black e6 base pawn and also to penetrate the 7th rank with Rf7. If it were Black's move, he would do the same type of thing: 1...cxd4 2.cxd4 Bb6 attacks the d4 base pawn and threatens penetration of the 2nd rank with 3...Rc2.

> **QUIZ 29.** In Diagram 102, it is Black's turn to play. White has a pawn chain on d4 and e5. How do you attack a pawn chain? How would you go about it here?

The Making of a Champion

I have talked about several players from history. One player you might be curious about, who is still alive today, is me! I'm only too happy to satisfy your curiosity.

I was born in Damascus in 1960. My father is Syrian and my mother English. When I was two years old, we moved to England; in 1967 we moved again, this time to the United States. We settled first in Seattle, Washington, then moved to the warmer climate of Virginia Beach, Virginia, and finally settled back in Seattle in 1972.

While in Virginia Beach, I got used to playing sports on fine, sunny days. The typical cold and rainy days of Seattle made me stir-crazy. When a neighbor offered to teach me chess, I jumped at the chance: anything to relieve the boredom of those long, wet evenings.

Yasser Seirawan: America's top player.

Those first chess lessons soon led me to the legendary Last Exit on Brooklyn coffee house, a chess haven where an unlikely bunch of unusual people congregates to do battle. There, I learned the ropes. When I got used to one player's crazed attacking style, I would sit down with a defensive player and force myself to learn to attack. This training paid off, and I quickly increased my skills.

After playing in tournaments for a few years, I finally became a master in 1977. I won the U.S. Junior Championship in 1978 and the World Junior Championship in 1979. With that victory (and the International Master title that came with it), I started receiving a steady stream of invitations to international events.

After tournaments in Sweden, England, and Holland, I was awarded the International Grandmaster title (the highest title other than World Champion) in 1980. At that time, I was the third youngest person in history to have received this title. Since that time, I have traveled to every corner of the world and my interest in chess has paid great dividends. With such feathers as the U.S. Chess Championship in my cap, I became the second American since Bobby Fischer to qualify for the World Championship matches. Presently, I am ranked 10th in the world and my main aspiration is to bring the World Champion title back to the United States.

Open Positions and Closed Positions

Most players think of themselves as attackers, so I will start by explaining open positions, which lend themselves to fast, aggressive games.

Open Positions

An open position has a minimum number of pawns sitting in the center. Pieces are not blocked and can zip into the enemy camp. As a result, attacks can be mounted quickly and often. To play an open position, getting your pieces out and your King castled into safety as quickly as possible is of utmost importance. In the absence of center pawns, the Rooks are able to enter the foray, often with devastating results.

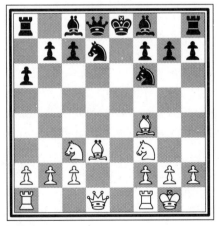

DIAGRAM 103.

The position shown in Diagram 103 is as open as possible, because all the center pawns have been traded. White has his army ready to move, and his King is safe. Black, on the other hand, is still trying to get his men out. Moreover, his King is still in the center and is vulnerable to the White Rooks and other White pieces. It is White's turn to play.

1.	Re1+	Be7
2.	Qe2!	

Excellent! White intensifies the pressure down the e-file and prevents Black from castling (because after castling White would eliminate Black's e7-Bishop with Qxe7). Notice how White's lead in development allows him to bring his Rooks into play, whereas Black's poor things on a8 and h8 are constrained and helpless.

2.	...	Nb6

Black blazes a trail for his c8-Bishop. He now hopes to play 3...Be6, which would close the e-file and allow him to castle.

3.	Rad1	

White's other Rook jumps to an open file. Now 3...Be6 would lose to 4.Bxa6! (which initiates a discovered attack by the Rook on d1) 4...Qc8 5.Bb5+. White would have a material advantage of 1 (a pawn). Black abandons 3...Be6 and plays

3.	...	Bd7

Black stops one threat but opens himself up to an even worse one. White now sees that, if he could draw the Black Queen away from the protection of the e7-Bishop, he would be able to checkmate his opponent.

4.	Bxc7!	Qxc7

For Black, it's either this move or 4...O-O, which would lead to 5.Bxd8 and an insurmountable 10 to 3 advantage in force for White. Even so, Black is doomed:

5.	Qxe7 checkmate	

Let that be a lesson to you: Castle quickly!

On occasion, a player may decide to play an opening gambit (sacrificing a pawn or two) to open up the center and gain a lead in development. Such was the case in a game between Lawrence Crakanthorp and Jonathan Maddox, played in New Zealand in 1933.

1. **e4** **c5**

Black is using what's called the *Sicilian Defense*. The idea is to control square d4 with a wing pawn so that if White plays a d4 advance, Black can trade the wing pawn for a more valuable center pawn.

2. **d4** **cxd4**
3. **Nf3**

White wants to recapture a pawn with his Knight rather than with his Queen, because the horse is much more comfortable in the center than the Queen would be. If instead of 3.Nf3 White plays 3.Qxd4, Black would gain valuable time by playing 3...Nc6, thereby attacking the White Queen. As it is, Black plays

3. **...** **e5**

Tricky but risky. Black hopes White will take the bait and play 4.Nxe5??, which would lose to 4...Qa5+ with a double attack on White's King and Knight. Black would then win a piece. The trouble with 3...e5 is that it does nothing for Black's development, it weakens his control of the important d5 central square, and it leaves the d7-pawn backward.

4. **c3!**

A good response. White sacrifices a pawn in order to open up the position and start an attack.

4. **...** **dxc3**
5. **Nxc3**

Now White's pieces jump nicely into the outpost on d5. Black must be very careful, because the position is open and White has a lead in development.

5. **...** **Nc6**

A good move. Black defends his e5-pawn and develops a piece.

6. **Bc4**

White develops another piece, controls d5, and eyes the vulnerable f7 point in Black's camp. Note how powerful the Bishop is on square c4. In general, Bishops fare better than Knights in open positions, because few of the pawns in the middle can block their way. Because Bishops are long-range pieces, they can penetrate deep into the enemy camp with just one move. Knights have a shorter range and often need to make two or three moves to position themselves for hostile action.

6. ... Be7??

This move leads to disaster, but a move like 6...Nf6 would also have created unsolvable problems after 7.Ng5!, when Black's f7-pawn falls.

7. Qd5

Oops! White threatens 8.Qxf7 checkmate, and Black can't save himself with 7...Nh6 because a response of 8.Bxh6 would simply repeat the threat of f7 checkmate. Black has to give his King room to run.

7.	**...**	**Qc7**	**9.**	**Qxg7**
8.	**Qxf7+**	**Kd8**		

A sobering move. White now has a 1-point material advantage and intends to increase it to 6 points with 10.Qxh8.

9. ... Bf6

Black defends the Rook but leaves his King wide open.

10. Qf8 checkmate

Black lost the game because he weakened control of an important central square, which the White Queen used as a point of entry into Black's position. He also fell behind in development, which allowed White to attack with superior force.

Closed Positions

We have seen that open games often lead to wild and woolly battles. A much slower type of game results from closed positions. A closed position is one in which the center is filled with pawns, which block the pieces and force both sides to slowly maneuver around the pawn walls to get their armies out.

DIAGRAM 104.

In Diagram 104, the center is completely blocked by pawns—a truly closed position. Play will focus on the wings. Black has a space advantage on the Kingside, so he will attack on that side, whereas White controls more space on the Queenside, so he will attack on that side. The principle at work here is

Attack where you have most space to maneuver.

In closed positions, you must also work hard to create open files for your Rooks. In Diagram 104, White will play for a c4-c5 advance followed by a capture on d6 with cxd6. This dual-purpose plan leads to the opening of the c-file for White's Rooks and forces Black's base to d6. Black will open up the g-file with ...g5-g4 followed by ...gxf3, which attacks the base of White's pawn chain.

To clear lines for your pieces in closed positions, you must start with pawn attacks. Contrast this strategy with that for open positions, in which the pieces lead the attack.

One more tip: Knights are often better than Bishops in closed positions. Knights can jump over other pieces and are not blocked by the pawns in their way, whereas Bishops hate walls of pawns. These walls block them and keep them locked up in their prison cells. In Diagram 105, the pathetic White

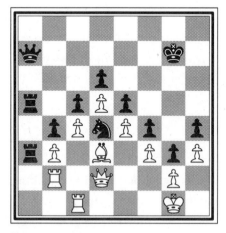

DIAGRAM 105.

Bishop is imprisoned by its own pawns, and Black's Knight is a real bone in White's throat. The Knight has penetrated the heart of White's position and will torment him for a long time to come. The fact that Black also controls the only open file (remember the importance of open files in closed positions) makes this game extremely unpleasant for White.

So which do I recommend for the beginning player: closed or open positions? Open positions, by all means! The type of game produced by open positions will teach you about timing and will introduce you to the tactics necessary to deal with lack of development and an exposed King. In general, closed positions are played more effectively by players with several years' experience under their belts. Of course, you will, on occasion, find yourself faced with a closed position. Don't panic. The suggestions I've given should enable you to handle such positions in an intelligent manner. Combine these suggestions with some experience and you will be able to play both types of game with skill.

QUIZ 30. Which statement is false?

- Closed positions tend to kccp out the enemy pieces and allow you to develop at a slower pace.
- Usually, you can safely postpone castling for quite a while in open positions.
- Knights generally perform better than Bishops in closed positions.

The Great Endgame Players

Though players such as Alexander Alekhine and Mikhail Tal made their fortunes with sparkling sacrifices and crowd-pleasing tricks, other great players have chosen less ostentatious paths. Take, for example, the

Paul Keres, the great Estonian Grandmaster.

Estonian Grandmaster Paul Keres (1916–75). When he started playing chess, he was a wild man. He ended almost every game with some sort of exciting attack. In addition to playing every game he could, he honed his attacking skills by playing postal chess, in which the opponents send each other one move at a time, written on a postcard. Though a game can take years to finish, postal chess sharpens your analytical abilities and is indispensable for isolated chess players. Keres had as many as 150 games on the go at once!

Making his mark in tournaments, Keres eventually climbed to the top. Though he was feared as an attacking genius, his style slowly began to change. Eventually, a new Keres emerged. He preferred a quieter, classical type of game and was extremely proficient at the endgame. He was happy to trade pieces and then win in the final stages of play.

Is this propensity for the endgame unusual? Not at all! Modern Grandmasters are well aware that the endgame is every bit as important as the opening and the middlegame. Players like Akiba Rubinstein (1882–1961), Emanuel Lasker (1868–1941), José Capablanca, Vasily Smyslov (1921–), and Tigran Petrosyan are all well known for their phenomenal mastery of this phase of the game.

Should the beginner focus on endgame strategy? No. Learn the basic principles of the endgame, but don't be overly concerned with mastering the endgame just now. Instead, attack at every opportunity (but only after all your pieces are developed) and be brutal about finishing off your opponent any way you can. If he avoids a checkmate, then take off all his pieces. When you have three or four pieces and he has only a King, you don't have to worry about an endgame. Enjoy the rout!

Pawn Structures in the Endgame

We have seen how different pawn structures affect the nature of play in the opening or middlegame. In the same ways, pawn structures affect the endgame.

Diagram 106 shows a typical closed position. White has an impotent Bishop blocked on the same color as its own pawns, whereas Black has a powerfully centralized Knight. To make matters worse for White, the Black King will be able to make inroads into White's camp. This point is very important. In an endgame, Kings become powerful pieces and must be rushed into the battle. In this case, Black's King and Knight can join forces and surround the enemy pawn on c4. One final advantage for Black is the fact that his g3-pawn is so far advanced. If Black can somehow get the g2-pawn out of the way, he will be able to move his g3-pawn and perhaps promote it to a Queen. To-gether, these factors add up to a losing cause for White.

It is Black's turn to play, and he wastes no time in rushing his King into the battle area.

1. ... Kb7

Having noticed that the White pawn on c4 cannot be defended by any other pawns, Black hastens to attack it.

2. Kf1

DIAGRAM 106.

White tries to bring his King up for defense, but he will arrive too late.

2.	...	Kb6		4.	Kd2
3.	Ke1	Kc5			

White could try to stay put, but he would eventually be pushed back by the superior Black forces. The play would go something like this: 4.Be2 Kb4 5.Bf1 Kc3 6.Kd1 Nc2! (the Black Knight is headed for an even better square on e3—remember, Knights are at their peak of strength on the 6th rank) 7.Ke2 (or 7.Kc1 Ne3, and if the Bishop moves, 8...Nxg2 provides the finishing touch) 7...Kxc4, and Black has won a pawn. Notice how ineffective the White Bishop is, whereas the Black Knight could hop to all sorts of vantage points.

4.	...	Nxf3+!

Black hopes to promote his pawn after 5.gxf3 g2 with 6...g1=Q. White does not oblige him:

5.	Kc3	Ng5

The nimble Knight runs rings around the Bishop. Now the Bishop can't move to f1 or e2 because of the threat of 6...Nxe4+.

6.	Bc2

If White plays 6.Kd2, Black would have the additional option of increasing his King's potential with 6...Kd4. As it is, he plays

6.	...	Nxh3!

He is still hoping for 7.gxh3 g2 and the crowning of a new Queen. Another strong Black move is 6...f3!, which breaks White's blockade on g2.

7.	Kd3	f3!

A Queen is certainly in the making, because any capture by the White pawn on g2 will be met with 8...g2 followed by 9...g1=Q. White resigns.

Now let's look at a vastly different picture. In Diagram 107, we
have a wide open board with
passed pawns on both sides. Because the White Bishop isn't
blocked by pawns, such a position
tends to work in favor of the player
with the Bishop.

DIAGRAM 107.

   1.   Be6!

White stops Black's pawn dead in
its tracks and prevents Black's
Knight from going to d5 or c4. This
move demonstrates why the Bishop's long-range powers are so highly
regarded. Because White now threatens to advance and promote his own
pawns, Black must make an effort to stop them. Unfortunately for Black,
the short-range Knight is not very good at such duties.

   1.   ...   Nd7

   2.   h5

White is not tempted by 2.Bxd7??, because Black would then be free to
advance his pawn with 2...a2.

   2.   ...   Nf8

   3   Ba2

White thwarts Black's attempt to take the White Bishop.

   3.   ...   b5   5.   g7

   4.   g6   b4

And the White pawn is headed for a promotion. This time, the White
Bishop completely dominated the poor Black horse!

QUIZ 31. In an endgame should you:

■ Continue to defend your King?

■ Bring out your King to join in the battle?

Tests

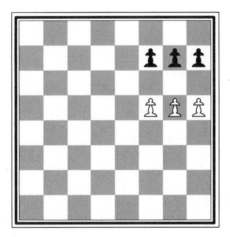

TEST 20. It is White's turn to play. Can White promote one of his pawns to a Queen?

TEST 21. Black has a passed pawn on d5 and a backward pawn on c6. White has doubled pawns on the b-file. Which side would you prefer to play?

TEST 22. It is Black's turn to play. Because his Queen is attacked by the White Knight, Black decides to capture the Knight with 1...Nxe5. White now has three ways to recapture. Which is best?

TEST 23. It is Black's turn to play, and he is a pawn ahead. Which side has a better chance of winning?

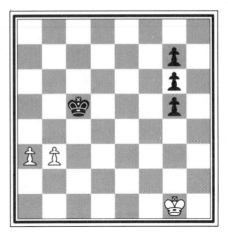

TEST 24. It is Black's turn to play. Though 1...0-0 is a good move, Black elects to play 1...Nbd7 first. Is it a bad idea for Black to postpone castling in this position?

Annotated Games

After learning the basic principles demonstrated in this book, you should practice by playing as much as possible. If you live in a ghost town or if everyone in your community thinks that chess is the part of your anatomy where your heart resides, consider buying a chess computer. These gadgets sell for as little as $90, and they're getting cheaper all the time. A computer is a perfect opponent. You can set its skill level and demand a game at any time—it never says "No."

When you have had a chance to get some games under your belt and have developed a good feel for the information I've given you, start examining a few master games. You will find the moves of particular games chronicled in weekly chess sections in newspapers or in books about the lives and games of particular players. In the meantime, this chapter gives you a taste of annotated games. Play through these games to see how the principles I've discussed are used in actual combat.

The Danger of Not Developing Your Pieces

Game 1: N.N.–Alphonse Goetz, Strassburg, 1880

(N.N. designates an unknown player, usually someone who has not yet made a mark in the world of chess.)

1. e4

White stakes a claim in the center. He frees his f1-Bishop and Queen.

1.   ...   e5

Black counters by grabbing an equal share of the center.

2.   f4

This old opening (called the *King's Gambit*) is rarely seen nowadays. White sacrifices a pawn so that he can pull Black's center pawn off to the side. This tactic will give White two center pawns to Black's one. White's goal is to get a big share of the center and, while Black is busy defending his extra pawn, White will obtain a lead in development. The one flaw in this plan is that it weakens White's King by allowing one of its protecting pawns to be captured.

2.   ...   exf4

3.   b3??

A horrible move! White should be developing his pieces. Because Black threatens to play 3...Qh4+, White should have played 3.Nf3. Then the game might have continued with 3...d6 4.d4 (by which White would threaten to capture a pawn with 5.Bxf4) 4...g5 5.Bc4, and White would have had a lead in development.

3.   ...   Qh4+

Usually, you don't want to move your Queen out so early. Here, however, Black's move presents White with two very bad choices: Either put the White King on a horrible square or give away more material.

4.   g3??

A better move is 4.Ke2, though Black would retain the advantage, because he has an extra pawn and the White King is stuck in the middle. (By moving his King, White forfeited the right to castle.)

4.   ...   fxg3

This pawn is going on quite a journey! White cannot capture it because after 5.hxg3, Black would play 5.Qxh1 and be a Rook (5 points) ahead.

5.   h3?

White has already lost, but this move leads to a comic finish.

5.	...	g2 discovered check
6.	Ke2	Qxe4+
7.	Kf2	

Now Black could win easily with 7...gxh1=Q, which gives him an 11-point material advantage. However, he sees something even better: under-promotion.

| 7. | ... | gxh1=N checkmate |

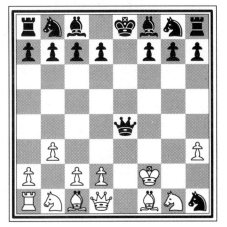

DIAGRAM 108.

As you can see in Diagram 108, in this position the Knight is stronger than a Queen. The underpromotion results in a slaughter. White weakened his King and didn't bother to develop any of his pieces. I hope his pitiful fate will scare you into getting your pieces out as quickly as possible!

Game 2: John Odin Howard Taylor–N.N., London, 1862

1.	e4	e5
2.	Nf3	

With this popular move, White attacks Black's pawn and develops a piece.

| 2. | ... | Nf6 |

Black plays what is called the *Petroff Defense*, hoping to get a symmetrical position after both sides exchange their e-pawns.

| 3. | Bc4 | |

White decides to set up an attack. He shows that he is willing to sacrifice a pawn in order to take a lead in development.

| 3. | ... | Nxe4 |

151

Black accepts the challenge!

    4.   Nc3

White is consistently bringing out his army. He avoids 4.Nxe5 d5, which would allow Black to attack White's Bishop with a gain of time.

    4.   ...   Nc5?

Black falls apart. By moving this Knight a third time, he allows White to take a large lead in development. A better move is 4...Nxc3, which would force White to take the time to capture the Black Knight and even the score. This point is important: If you have to move a piece and thereby lose time, try to capture an enemy piece equal in value to the one you're moving. Then your opponent must lose an equivalent amount of time to recapture.

    5.   Nxe5

White regains his lost material and also makes a threat against Black's f7-pawn.

    5.   ...   f6??

Suicide! When you are behind in development, you can rarely afford to weaken your King. Another really bad move is 5...Qe7?, which would lead to 6.O-O! Qxe5 7.Re1. Black's Queen would then be lost because it would be pinned to his King. Black should have blocked White's Bishop by moving his Knight yet again, with 5...Ne6. Then 6.d4 followed by 7.O-O would leave White with a dominating position, but at least Black could stay in the game for a while.

    6.   Qh5+

All of White's pieces now jump on the Black King, which finds itself forced on a long and unpleasant journey toward checkmate.

    6.   ...   g6
    7.   Bf7+   Ke7
    8.   Nd5+   Kd6

Diagram 109 shows the current position. When you find yourself moving nothing but your King, you know that something has gone terribly wrong!

9. Nc4+

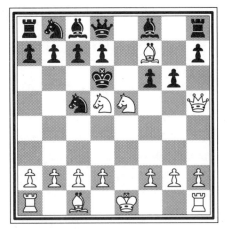

DIAGRAM 109.

Always working with checks, White does not give Black a moment to catch his breath.

9. ... Kc6

10. Nb4+ Kb5

11. a4+

White sacrifices a Knight in order to draw the Black King off on a mission from which it will never return. In general, you will find that when a King is drawn into enemy territory early in the game, it is destined to be quickly checkmated.

11. ... Kxb4

12. c3+ Kb3

Ever since move 7, every one of Black's moves has been his only legal option.

13. Qd1 checkmate

Diagram 110 shows how completely White has managed to surround the Black King.

DIAGRAM 110.

The Danger of Bringing Out the Queen Too Early

Game 3: Persifor Frazer–Jean Taubenhaus, Paris, 1888

1.	e4	e5
2.	Nf3	Nc6

Black knows the best reply. He develops a piece and simultaneously defends his pawn on e5.

3.	d4	

This move (called the *Scotch Opening*) is no longer popular, because White will lose a tempo recapturing the pawn on d4.

3.	...	exd4

A good decision.

4.	Nxd4	Qh4

Black goes hunting for the White pawn on e4. This tactic is risky, because the Black Queen will become vulnerable to attack from White's pieces.

5.	Nc3	Nf6?

Black's move is not consistent with his previous plays. He should have tried 5...Bb4, which would pin White's c3-Knight (the lone defender of the e4-pawn) and renew his threat against the pawn on e4.

6.	Nf5	

Suddenly, Black's Queen is no longer the hunter but the hunted!

6.	...	Qh5
7.	Be2	

White continues to develop pieces and at the same time mounts an attack against the Queen.

7.	...	Qg6
8.	Nh4	

This attack on the Black Queen leaves it with nowhere to go. Squares h6 and g5 are controlled by White's c1-Bishop, and squares h5 and g4 are under surveillance by the e2-Bishop. The e4-pawn is defended by the c3-Knight, and the g2-pawn is defended by the h4-Knight. Because White will capture his Queen on the next move, Black resigns the game.

The moral: Don't move your Queen too early. First, get your pawns and minor pieces out. Next, castle as soon as you can. Finally, find homes for your Rooks and Queen.

Game 4: Otto Kraus–Victor Costin, correspondence, 1914

1. d4

This move is just as good as 1.e4. White frees both his c1-Bishop and his Queen, gets a pawn in the center, and pressures the important e5 square.

1. ... c5

Not the most common move. Black usually plays 1...d5 (copying White) or 1...Nf6 (developing and controlling e4 and d5). Black's plan with 1...c5 is to trade White's center pawn for a less valuable wing pawn.

2. dxc5

White forces Black to consider how he is going to recapture a pawn. Another good move for White is 2.d5, which would gain space.

2. ... Qa5+

Black immediately wins back the pawn, but brings out his Queen too early. A better move would be 2...e6 followed by 3...Bxc5, or even 2...Na6 followed by 3...Nxc5. In both cases, the advanced minor piece would be much more useful than the advanced and exposed Black Queen.

3. Nc3

White calmly blocks the check and develops his Knight to a good square.

3. ... Qxc5

Black has regained his pawn, but his Queen is not completely safe on c5.

4. e4

An excellent move. Now White has a center pawn controlling square d5, and both of his Bishops are ready to be developed.

4. ... e5?

Simply awful! Black compounds his lack of development by weakening his control of the central squares. This move leaves a gaping hole on d5 and turns the pawn on d7 into a backward pawn. Better moves are 4...Nc6, 4...Nf6, or even 4...e6, which would free the f8-Bishop and keep White's Knight out of d5.

5. Nf3

White brings out another piece and eyes the e5-pawn hungrily.

5. ... d6

Though the e5-pawn is already guarded by the Queen, Black decides to give the pawn some additional support. Such consideration would be fine if Black had more pieces out, but he is falling more and more behind in development and should be trying to catch up!

6. Nd5

White places his Knight powerfully in the center and at the same time sets a trap. Also a good move is 6.Be3, which develops another piece with a gain of time, because Black's Queen would be forced to move again.

6. ... Ne7

Black finally develops a Knight and offers to trade his conservative horse for the strong White counterpart on d5. Unfortunately for Black, he has fallen right into White's trap!

7. b4!

Suddenly, Black's Queen has very few squares to retreat to.

7. ... Qc6

The only safe port.

8. Bb5!

White pins Black's Queen to his King but leaves the White Bishop without protection. Has White lost his senses?

8.   ...   Qxb5

If the Black Queen doesn't take the White Bishop, the Bishop will take the Queen.

9.   Nc7+

The point of White's play is now clear. This Knight fork initiates a double attack on Black's King and Queen. Because the Black Queen will be captured with White's next move, Black decides to resign the game.

The Danger of Leaving Your Pieces Undefended

Game 5: Kaprinay–Hans Hubner, correspondence, 1926

1.   c4

White plays the *English Opening*. As well as giving his Queen some freedom, White hopes to gain control of square d5 by placing his Knight on c3 (which together with the c4-pawn points two attackers at d5) and his f1-Bishop on g2. This opening has been used by all the great players at one time or another, including Bobby Fischer and the present World Champion, Garry Kasparov.

1.   ...   e5

A good reply. Black counters by staking a claim to the d4 square.

2.   Nc3

White increases his control of d5, hits the e4 central square, and develops a piece.

2.   ...   Nc6

Black increases his control of d4, defends the e5-pawn, and also develops a piece. So far, Black is playing well.

3.   g3

White intends to fianchetto his Bishop. On g2, the Bishop will control the long h1-a8 diagonal and, in particular, it will reinforce White's control of d5 and e4.

    3.   ...   Nf6

Another good move by Black. He develops his remaining Knight and tries to counter White's control of squares e4 and d5.

    4.   Bg2   Bb4

Black develops his Bishop and prepares to castle. He also intends to compromise White's pawns with 5...Bxc3, forcing White to recapture with 6.bxc3 or 6.dxc3. In either case, White's pawns would be doubled. So far, Black has played in exemplary fashion.

    5.   Nd5

White moves his Knight a second time, placing it on the advanced d5 post. More common is 5.Nf3, which would continue piece development and prepare the way for castling.

    5.   ...   Nxd5

Not bad, but continued development with 5...O-O would be preferable. After 5...O-O 6.Nxb4 Nxb4, material would be even, and Black would enjoy a lead in development.

    6.   cxd5

By threatening Black's Knight, White forces it to move and gains time. Though White has doubled his pawns, the pawn on d5 cramps Black, and the resulting opening of the c-file gives White a nice home for his Rooks later in the game. (Remember, Rooks belong on open files.)

White could also have played 6.Bxd5, but that move would put no pressure on Black, who would just ignore it and castle, with good development as the outcome.

    6.   ...   Nd4??

At first glance, this move seems quite good. The problem is that Black has left an unprotected piece on b4 and that his Knight is a target for attack on d4. An even worse move is 6...Na5??, leading to 7.Qa4 Qe7 (defending the Bishop on b4) 8.a3. Then if Black's Bishop moves out of danger, the Knight on a5 would be lost. Black should have played 6...Ne7, which would safeguard all his pieces.

7. e3

White attacks the Knight again and forces it into an undefended position.

7. ... Nf5

Black's choices are limited. Squares e6 and c6 are covered by the White pawn on d5. Squares f3, e2, c2, and b3 are all covered by the White Queen (and other pieces). Black's only other move is 7...Nb5, but then 8.Qa4 would attack the Knight and the Bishop simultaneously and doom one of them to destruction.

8. Qg4!

The White Queen attacks both the Black Bishop on b4 and the Black Knight on f5. Because Black has no way of guarding both pieces, he must lose material. Disgusted with himself, Black resigns.

The moral: Take special care of an advanced piece that is undefended or you will lose it.

Game 6: Computer–N.N., Seattle, 1989

1. e4 e5

2. Nf3 Nf6

We saw this move—the Petroff Defense—earlier, in Game 2. Black hopes to copy White's moves and gain an equal position.

3. Nxe5 Nxe4?

Black's desire to regain material is understandable, but he walks into a trap. You must be especially careful when you place a piece far from the security of the rest of your army. Black's best move is first to play 3...d6! and only after 4.Nf3 to play Nxe4, because 5.Qe2 would then be comfortably countered with 5...Qe7.

4. Qe2

White threatens to eat the Black Knight. White also has designs against the Black King, which is sitting uncomfortably on the same file as the White Queen.

4. ... d5

A good move. Black defends his Knight and frees his c8-Bishop.

5. d3

White attacks the poor Knight again.

5. ... Nf6??

Black is oblivious to White's true threat. Black should have played 5...Qe7 so that after 6.dxe4 Qxe5 7.exd5 Qxe2+ 8.Bxe2, White would be ahead by only a pawn. Instead, after 5...Nf6 the roof caves in.

6. Nc6 discovered check

By this discovered check, White's Queen attacks Black's King while White's Knight attacks Black's Queen, all at the same time!

6. ... Qe7

Any other move loses the Queen to 7.Nxd8.

7. Nxe7 Bxe7

8. Bg5

The wily computer develops his Bishop and threatens to disrupt Black's pawn structure with 9.Bxf6, because the pin on the e7-Bishop would force Black to play 9...gxf6.

8. ... O-O

Black sees a little trick, but it turns out that the only person tricked is himself!

9. Qxe7! Re8

Black will regain a Queen, but White will still end up ahead by a Rook and a Bishop. White is up 9 points now; he will be up by 8 points after the trades. White is willing to part with a point in order to trade several pieces and simplify the position.

10. Bxf6!   Rxe7+

11. Bxe7

Now White's strategy is to trade Black's last three pieces, leaving White free to do as he pleases with his remaining men.

11. ...   Nc6

Black develops his Knight and attacks the e7-Bishop.

12. Bg5   Nb4

Black threatens to fork White on c2.

13. Na3

White stops the threat and develops a piece.

13. ...   Bf5

14. Kd2

Because this is the endgame, White is happy to leave his King in the center, where it can help the other pieces.

14. ...   Re8

15. c3

Black doesn't have enough pieces left to sustain any kind of attack, so White now drives Black's Knight back.

15. ...   Nc6

16. d4

White gains space and at the same time takes control of square e5 away from the Black Knight.

16. ...   Kf8

17. Bf4

White's Bishop attacks the pawn on c7.

17. ...   Re7

18. Bd3

White sticks with his plan of trading pieces. Another good move is 18.Nb5, which would attack the c7-pawn.

18.   ...   Bxd3

19.   Kxd3   a6

Black keeps White's Knight from moving to b5.

20.   Rhe1

White continues his trading policy.

20.   ...   Rxe1

21.   Rxe1   Nd8

Black has no way to defend the c7-pawn.

22.   Bxc7   Ne6

23.   Bg3   Ke8

24.   Nc2

It's time to put the Knight to work. Remember, don't play with only one or two pieces. Use all of your army!

24.   ...   Kd7

25.   Nb4

The White Knight attacks the d5-pawn and prevents the Black King from coming to the pawn's defense by moving to c6.

25.   ...   Nc7

26.   Bxc7

Success! All of Black's pieces are gone. His King and remaining pawns cannot hope to withstand the power of White's Rook and Knight.

26.   ...   Kxc7

27.   Re7+

This move is even stronger than 27.Nxd5+. White's Rook will now eat everything in its path.

27.	...	Kd6	30.	Rxg7	Ke6
28.	Rxf7	a5	31.	Rxh7	Kf5
29.	Nc2	b6	32.	Rh6	

Note how helpless Black is. In fact, Black's cause is completely hopeless, but he plays until the bitter end.

32.	...	b5	35.	Nxb4	Kg5
33.	Rb6	b4	36.	Nxd5	
34.	cxb4	axb4			

Black's army is completely wiped out! Now all that remains is for White to checkmate the King.

36.	...	Kf5
37.	f3	

Also effective is for White to advance his a-pawn and crown a new Queen. Checkmate would then be easy. But White sees a more satisfying finale.

37.	...	Kg5	39.	h3	Kg5
38.	g3	Kf5	40.	h4+	Kf5

Black can also play 40...Kh5, leading to 41.Nf4 checkmate.

41.	g4 checkmate

As this game shows, capturing all your opponent's pieces can be a most effective way of winning the battle.

The Danger of Weakening Your King's Position

Game 7: Frank Melville Teed–Eugene Delmar, New York, 1896

1.	d4	f5

This move is called the *Dutch Defense*. Black wants to place his Knight behind the f5-pawn and exert maximum pressure on square e4. The one slight drawback to this opening is that it opens the h5-e8 diagonal and exposes the Black King.

2. Bg5

A sharp reply. White pins the Black pawn on e7 and goads Black into advancing his Kingside pawns, thereby weakening the Black King's position.

2. ... h6

Black takes the bait! Notice how more and more holes are developing around the Black King. Those holes may eventually serve as entry points for the White pieces.

3. Bh4

White retreats out of danger while continuing to pin the e7-pawn.

3. ... g5

Black thinks he is going to capture White's Bishop. Encircling tactics often do win material, but in this case, Black's weakened Kingside interferes with his materialistic plans.

4. Bg3

The White Bishop has no other place to go.

4. ... f4

Black traps the Bishop.

5. e3!

A rude shock. White makes a double threat: 6.Qh5 checkmate or 6.exf4, saving the Bishop and winning a pawn.

5. ... h5

Black neutralizes the 6.Qh5 threat and intends to meet 6.exf4 with 6...h4, which renews the attack on the Bishop.

6. Bd3

The other White Bishop takes advantage of a hole in the Black camp. Now White threatens 7.Bg6 checkmate.

6. ... Rh6

Black thinks he has stopped the checkmate and will finally capture the g3-Bishop. A surprise awaits him.

7.   Qxh5+!!

White draws the Black Rook away from its control of g6.

7.   ...   Rxh5

8.   Bg6 checkmate

Game 8: Zeissl–Walter Von Walthoffen, Vienna, 1898

1.   e4   e5

2.   Nf3   Nc6

3.   Bb5

This is the *Ruy López Opening*, one of the oldest and most respected openings. White quickly develops his Kingside pieces and prepares to castle, while pressuring Black's pawn on e5.

3.   ...   f5

A sharp but risky response. Black attacks White in the center but weakens his King position at the same time. Safer moves are 3...Nf6 or 3...a6. Note that after 3...a6 White would not win a pawn with 4.Bxc6 dxc6 5.Nxe5, because with Qd4, Black counterattacks both White's Knight and the e4-pawn.

4.   d4

White avoids 4.exf5 e4, because his Knight would get kicked around. The best move here is 4.Nc3, which would develop a piece and defend the pawn on e4.

4.   ...   fxe4

Black forces White to move his Knight and make some attempt to regain his lost pawn.

5.   Nxe5

Material is once again equal.

5.   ...   Nxe5

6.   dxe5   c6!

Material is still equal after the trades. However, the White Bishop is now under attack and White must move it to a place of safety. The problem is Black's hidden threat to pick up White's pawn on e5.

7.   Bc4

White gives up a pawn for nothing. A better fighting chance is 7.Nc3! cxb5 8.Nxe4. Though White would be 2 points behind, he would have a lead in development, more space, and chances for attack. For example, 8...d5 would lose another pawn to 9.exd6 e.p. (remember, *e.p.* stands for *en passant*), and the developing 8...Ne7 would run into 9.Nd6 checkmate.

7.   ...   Qa5+

A double attack. Black hits White's King and the e5-pawn.

8.   Nc3   Qxe5

Black is now 1 point ahead. What makes matters really bad for White is that Black pawns firmly control the center, restricting the movement of White's army.

9.   O-O   d5

Black gains space and time, because White is forced to sound the retreat for his Bishop.

10.   Bb3   Nf6

Black pays special attention to time now that he has the advantage in space and force.

11.   Be3

White has a lead in development, but Black's center pawns effectively block the White pieces.

11.   ...   Bd6

A very strong move. Black develops a piece, prepares to castle, and threatens to checkmate White with 12...Qxh2.

12.   g3

A terrible move, because it creates holes in the White King's position. Here, however, White has no choice, because Black would counter the other possibility, 12.f4, with exf4 e.p. The ...Qxh2 would still be a threat, and the e3-Bishop would be attacked. Black has forced White to weaken his Kingside—a strategy well worth copying!

12. ...   Bg4!

The problem with weakening squares is that enemy pieces tend to head toward them. When Black sees that f3 has been weakened (no White pawn can defend it), he hastens to plant a piece there. The fact that he can develop at the same time is a bonus for Black.

13. Qd2   Bf3

As you can see in Diagram 111, the holes around White's King allow Black's pieces to infiltrate. Drafty positions of this kind often give rise to a quick and violent checkmate.

14. Bf4

White attacks both Black's Queen and Bishop, hoping to trade a piece or two and ease his defensive burden. This strategy is usually a good one for the defender, but here it is simply too late.

DIAGRAM 111.

14. ...   Qh5!

If White captures the Bishop, he will be checkmated, because 15.Bxd6 would lead to Qh3, followed by 16...Qg2 checkmate.

15. Nd1

White brings his Knight around to defend square g2 and attempt to stave off checkmate.

15. ...   Qh3

Another Black piece penetrates White's position. Now 16...Qg2 checkmate is threatened.

16. Ne3

White stops the checkmate.

16. ...   Ng4!

Still another Black piece joins the attack. This time, 17...Qxh2 checkmate is the threat.

17. Rfe1

White tries to create an escape for his King. Another possible move, 17.Nxg4, would lead to 17...Qg2 checkmate.

17. ...   Qxh2+

18. Kf1   Qh1 checkmate

This horrible rout was made possible by the holes in White's Kingside, which invited the Black pieces to penetrate White's position.

The Satisfaction of Learning

Congratulations! You've just played through a number of chess games that featured many classical lessons. Learn these lessons well, and you will suffer fewer losses on your road to chess mastery.

Chapter Seven

The Four Principles and You

M ost beginners find the idea of calculating a string of chess moves on the fly terrifying—they feel they just can't do it. Actually, lots of players with a good deal of experience behind them feel the same way. Don't worry about it! Being able to accurately calculate moves comes only after you understand and practice the basic principles of the game. Force, time, space, and pawn structure: These are the elements you should work on. When you have a thorough grasp of these four principles, calculating which moves to make and when to make them will become a cinch.

Some top players prefer to strategically assess their games in terms of the four principles, even though they have the knowledge and experience to make rapid calculations. As an example, let's go back to the 1960 World Championship match between Mikhail Botvinnik (the champion) and Mikhail Tal (the challenger).

For many years, Botvinnik had ruled world chess. His style was profoundly strategic, but aggressive. Whenever possible, he would come to decisions using the principles that we have studied in this book. Tal, on the other hand, was famous for his ability to calculate long strings of moves with amazing rapidity. During one game, Tal was on the attack. Botvinnik, thinking for a long time, decided on the correct defensive strategy and drew the game. Afterwards, Tal listed a huge series of move

---

QUIZ 32. Which statement is false?

■ You should calculate every possible move and counter-move.

■ Calculating moves is useful, but applying general principles so that you can recognize potential weaknesses is just as important.

---

variations, thinking that Botvinnik had arrived at the correct strategy by calculating the same possibilities. The young challenger was dumbfounded when the champion stated that he had decided on an overall strategy by weighing his position in the light of the principles—he had made very few calculations. The two different approaches had, however, led to the same solution!

By the way, Tal eventually won this match (best of 21 games) and became World Champion. However, one year later Botvinnik was granted a rematch and decisively won back his title.

Psychological Factors

It has often been said that people are their own worst enemies. The saying is particularly applicable to chess players. We can memorize all the openings; we can study the middlegame and master thousands of different positions; we can become endgame experts. But even with experience and significant accomplishments under our belts, we can still be influenced by psychological factors that inhibit the way we play. Let's look at the two biggest mental pitfalls: stress and lack of confidence.

Stress

Stress is the bane of the serious chess player. A game of tournament chess lasts several hours. If money or ego is on the line, the situation can become very stressful. As stress builds, thinking becomes clouded and nerves start to fray. Some people short-circuit altogether, making blunders they would never make under more casual circumstances.

Obviously, chess players must learn to keep calm. Deep breathing is a good method. Grandmaster Svetozar Gligoric used to eat chocolate throughout his games, following the advice of legendary World Champion Alexander Alekhine:

"A brain without sugar is not a brain."

To avoid becoming a sugar addict (not to mention obese), Fischer drank apple and orange juice throughout his games. Though juice has a high sugar content, it seems more healthy than pounds of chocolate!

Lack of Confidence

A chess player's confidence is only as solid as his last victory, and loss can transform him into an insecure wimp. If more losses follow, he becomes even more unsure of himself, creating a crisis of confidence that is hard to snap out of.

Only you can prevent this crisis from developing. If you lose, consider what you have learned from the experience and keep on playing. Apply the information I've given you in this book, and sooner or later you will start turning the tables, winning as many games as you lose.

Be prepared to lose and to win. In mastering anything, you're bound to have setbacks. Learn from your losses.

It's amazing what lack of confidence and the fear that comes with it can do. Suppose, for example, that a fairly low-rated player (White) is playing a well-known master (Black). White has a defeatist attitude from

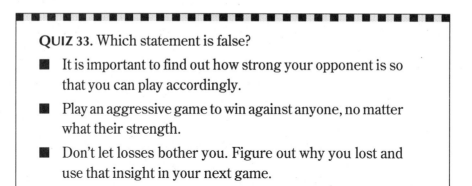

QUIZ 33. Which statement is false?

■ It is important to find out how strong your opponent is so that you can play accordingly.

■ Play an aggressive game to win against anyone, no matter what their strength.

■ Don't let losses bother you. Figure out why you lost and use that insight in your next game.

the beginning, and his thinking all along is, "I don't even need to analyze this move. If such a strong player makes this threat, then I know it must be good." Of course, Black wins the game without much difficulty.

Now suppose that White is playing a complete beginner or someone with a lower rating than himself. White looks long and hard for a way to win. Faced with exactly the same positions as in the first scenario, his thinking now goes like this: "I really want to beat this guy. If I take on d7, I threaten a Back Rank Mate. If he then plays 1...Qxh2+, I just step aside. He will soon run out of checks and I will win." Notice the change in attitude?

Don't change your approach to the game out of fear! Play aggressively to win against anyone, even the World Champion.

Photo Album

Chess is not just a sport for brainy intellectuals but for the masses! These four photographs show hundreds of players competing in the 1989 Software Toolworks Open Tournament.

In tournaments, chess clocks are used to time each player's moves. If a player fails to make the required number of moves in a specified period of time, he loses.

In tournament chess, each player keeps his own record of the
game. Later, the record will provide lessons on what to do or
not to do in the future.

In this ocean of chess players, note the empty chairs. Some
players are tardy! Chess players are notorious late risers.

In the U.S. Championship, America's strongest Grandmasters annually compete in a round robin. Moves are recorded on a demonstration board so that the audience can follow the games.

During the 1989–90 U.S. Championship, International Master Jack Peters lectures on the games in progress.

Yugoslavia's highest-ranked female chess player, Alisa Maric, studies her position.

Grandmasters Yasser Seirawan and Nick de Firmian engage in a Blitz game before the television cameras. In Blitz, each player has 5 minutes to complete the game. Blitz is one of the most popular forms of chess.

Grandmaster Maxim Dlugy probes the mysteries of his position.

The 1988–89 U.S. Women's Champion, Alexey Rudolph Root, flashes a winning smile.

Your author, masking his anxiety: "Oh boy, what am I going to do next?"

International Master Stuart Rachels pulled off the biggest upset of his career by tying for first place in the 1989–90 U.S. Championship.

Arthur Dake, a 75-year-old former U.S. Olympic team player,
still pushes the pieces.

Yasser Seirawan's first game against then-World Champion
Anatoly Karpov took place in Mar del Plata, Argentina in 1982.
Hundreds of spectators watched this 13-hour game, which was
played over two days. The final result was a draw. In this postmortem, Seirawan points out his crucial error.

Nana Alexandria, one of the Soviet Union's finest Woman Grandmasters (WGMs), performs a simultaneous exhibition. In this case, Alexandria plays 40 opponents.

Spectators crowd the simultaneous exhibition as Alexandria closes in for the kill.

A young Californian gets a private one-on-one lesson.

Alexandria gets a smile from her student.

Grandmaster Tony Miles (left) plays against the monster chess program Deep Thought. Note the portable computer, which is connected via modem to the supercomputers at Bell Laboratories.

Glossary

Active: In relation to an opponent's style, denotes a preference for aggressive or tactical types of play. Otherwise, means an aggressive move or position.

Advantage: A net superiority of position, usually based on force, time, space, or pawn structure.

Algebraic Notation: Many ways of writing chess moves have been devised over the years. In fact, there are probably as many ways of writing chess moves as there are languages. However, algebraic notation has become the international standard.

Essentially, each square on the chessboard is given a letter and a number. The files are assigned the letters a, b, c, d, e, f, g, and h, from left to right from White's perspective. The ranks are assigned the numbers 1, 2, 3, 4, 5, 6, 7, and 8, from bottom to top from White's perspective. Thus, the bottom left corner is square a1 and the top right corner is square h8.

When a piece travels from one square to another, algebraic notation enables you to identify the piece and the square to which it is moving. For example, if the Rook moves from square a1 to square a8, you write Ra8. For pawn moves, you write only the square to which the pawn moves; for example, e4. Castling Kingside is written O-O, and castling Queenside is written O-O-O. In this book, algebraic notation is sometimes referred to as *chess notation* or simply *notation*.

Analysis: The calculation of a series of moves based on a particular position. In tournament play, you are not allowed to move the pieces during analysis but must make all calculations in your head. When the game is over, opponents commonly analyze the game they have just played, moving the pieces about in an effort to discover what the best moves would have been. *See also* Postmortem.

Annotation: Written comments about a position or game. The comments can take the form of narrative, chess notation, or a combination of both.

Attack: To start an aggressive action in a particular area of the board, or to threaten to capture a piece or pawn.

Back Rank Mate: A checkmate where the King is confined to its back rank. For example, White's Rook is on a8; Black's King is on g8, with pawns on f7, g7, and h7.

Backward Pawn: A pawn that has fallen behind its comrades and can no longer be defended by another pawn. Usually considered a weakness.

Berserker: A playing style characterized by frenzied attacks with one or two pieces. Named after ancient Scandinavian warriors who worked themselves up into battle frenzies and then charged their opponents with little regard for strategy or personal danger.

Bind: When one player has a grip on the position because of a large advantage in space and his opponent is unable to find useful moves.

Bishop Pair: Two Bishops versus a Bishop and a Knight or two Knights. Two Bishops work well together because they can control diagonals of both colors. *See also* Opposite-Colored Bishops.

Blockade: To stop an enemy pawn by placing a piece (ideally a Knight) directly in front of it. Popularized by Aaron Nimzowitsch.

Blunder: A terrible move that loses material or involves decisive positional or tactical concessions.

Book: Opening analysis found in chess books and magazines. A *book player* relies heavily on memorization of published material rather than on his own creative spark.

Break: The offer of an exchange of pawns in order to gain space or mobility. Also called a *pawn break*.

Breakthrough: Denotes a penetration of the enemy position.

Brilliancy: A game that contains a stunning sacrifice or an amazing strategic concept. Sometimes such a game receives a special monetary award for excellence, called a *brilliancy prize*.

Calculation of Variations: The working out of chains of moves without physically moving the pieces.

Castle: A player castles by moving his King and Rook simultaneously. Castling is the only move in which a player can deploy two pieces in one move. Castling allows a player to move his King out of the center (the main theater of action in the opening) to the flank, where the King can be protected by pawns. Additionally, castling develops a Rook.

When White castles Kingside, he moves his King from e1 to g1 and his h1-Rook to f1. When Black castles Kingside, he moves his King from e8 to g8 and his h8-Rook to f8. When White castles Queenside, he moves his King from e1 to c1 and his a1-Rook to d1. And when Black castles Queenside, he moves his King from e8 to c8 and his a8-Rook to d8.

Center: The center is the area of the board encompassed by the rectangle c3-c6-f6-f3. Squares e4, d4, e5, and d5 are the most important part of the center. The e- and d-files are the *center files*.

Centralize: To place pieces and pawns in the center, or as close to the center as possible. From there, they can control a good chunk of enemy territory.

Checkmate: An attack against the enemy King from which the King cannot escape. When a player checkmates his opponent's King, he wins the game.

Classical: A style of play that focuses on the creation of a full pawn center. Classical principles tend to be rather dogmatic and inflexible. The philosophy of the classical players was eventually challenged by the so-called "hypermoderns." *See also* Hypermodern.

Closed Game: A position that is obstructed by blocking chains of pawns. Such a position tends to favor Knights over Bishops, because the pawns block the diagonals.

Combination: A calculable, tactical series of moves that usually involves a sacrifice.

Compensation: An advantage in one area that balances the opponent's advantage in another area. Material versus development is one example; three pawns versus a Bishop is another.

Connected Passed Pawns: Two or more passed pawns of the same color on adjacent files. *See also* Passed Pawns.

Control: To completely dominate an area of the board. Dominating a file or a square, or simply having the initiative, can constitute control.

Counterplay: When the player who has been on the defensive starts his own aggressive action.

Cramp: The lack of mobility that is the usual result of a disadvantage in space.

Critical Position: An important point in the game, where victory or defeat hangs in the balance.

Defense: A move or series of moves designed to thwart an enemy attack. Also used in the names of many openings initiated by Black. Examples are the French Defense and the Caro–Kann Defense.

Development: The process of moving pieces from their starting positions to new posts, from which they control a greater number of squares and have greater mobility.

Doubled Pawns: Two pawns of the same color lined up on a file. This doubling can only come about as the result of a capture.

Draw: A tied game. A draw can result from a stalemate, from a three-time repetition of position, or by agreement between the players. *See also* Stalemate; Three-Time Repetition of Position.

Dynamic: Implies action and movement. A dynamic factor concerns itself with actual moves and threats and involves combinations of attack and defense maneuvers. The two main aspects of a dynamic factor are time and force.

Elo Rating: The system by which players are rated. Devised by Professor Arpad Elo (1903–) of Milwaukee and adopted by FIDE in 1970. A beginner might have a 900 rating, the average club player 1600, a state champion 2300, and the World Champion 2800.

En Passant: A French term that means *in passing*. When a pawn advances two squares (which it can do only if it has not moved before) and passes an enemy pawn on an adjacent file that has advanced to its 5th rank, it can be captured by the enemy pawn as if it had moved only one square. The capture is optional and must be made at the first opportunity; otherwise, the right to capture that particular pawn under those particular circumstances is lost.

En Prise: A French term that means *in take*. It describes a piece or pawn that is vulnerable to capture.

Endgame: The third and final phase of a chess game. An endgame arises when few pieces remain on the board. The clearest signal that the ending is about to begin is when Queens are exchanged.

Equality: A situation in which neither side has an advantage or the players' advantages balance out.

Exchange: The trading of pieces, usually ones of equal value.

Exchange, The: *Winning the Exchange* means you have won a Rook (5 points) for a Bishop or a Knight (3 points).

Fianchetto: An Italian word that means *on the flank*. A fianchetto is placing a White Bishop on g2 or b2 or a Black Bishop on g7 or b7. Few players pronounce this word properly, the correct pronunciation being *fyan-KET-to*.

FIDE: The acronym for *Fédération Internationale des Échecs*, the international chess federation.

File: A vertical column of eight squares. Designated in algebraic notation as the a-file, b-file, and so on. *See also* Half-Open; Open.

Flank: The a-, b-, and c-files on the Queenside, and the f-, g-, and h-files on the Kingside. *Flank openings* start with moves on the flanks (such as

1.b3, 1.c4, and 1.Nf3) and usually involve a fianchetto and attempts to control the center squares with pawns and pieces from the flanks.

Force: Material. An advantage in force arises when one player has more material than his opponent or when he outmans his opponent in a certain area of the board.

Forced: A move or series of moves that must be played to avoid disaster.

Forfeit: *See* Time Control. A less common way to forfeit is to arrive for a game more than an hour after it was scheduled to start.

Gambit: The voluntary sacrifice of at least a pawn in the opening, with the idea of gaining a compensating advantage (usually time, which permits development).

General Principles: The fundamental rules of chess, devised to enable less advanced players to react logically to different positions. Also used more often than you would think by Grandmasters!

Ghost: The illusion of a threat. Fear of the opponent or an overly nervous disposition can easily lead to the "perception" of ghosts.

Grandmaster: A title awarded by FIDE to players who meet an established set of performance standards, including a high Elo rating. It is the highest title (other than World Champion) attainable in chess. A separate Woman Grandmaster title is awarded to distinguished women chess players. Lesser titles are International Master and FIDE Master, which is the lowest title awarded for international play. Once earned, a Grandmaster title cannot be taken away. *See also* Elo Rating; Master.

Grandmaster Draw: A quick, uninteresting draw between two Grandmasters. Nowadays, this term is applied to a quick draw between any class of player.

Half-Open: A file that contains none of one player's pawns, but one or more of the opponent's.

Hang: To be unprotected and exposed to capture.

Hanging Pawns: A pawn island consisting of two pawns side by side on the 4th rank on half-open files. Sometimes, hanging pawns are the source of dynamic energy for an attack; at other times, they become a target, subject to frontal attack by the enemy. *See also* Pawn Island.

Hold: To avoid defeat. To stave off loss. However, to *hold out* is to offer tough resistance, but to eventually lose against a better play. A move that would *hold the position* is one that would most likely allow a successful defense.

Hole: A square that cannot be defended by a pawn. Such a square makes an excellent home for a piece, because the piece cannot be chased away by hostile pawns.

Hypermodern: A school of thought that arose in reaction to the classical theories of chess. The hypermoderns insisted that putting a pawn in the center in the opening made it a target. The heroes of this movement were Richard Réti and Aaron Nimzowitsch, both of whom expounded the idea of controlling the center from the flanks. Like the ideas of the classicists, those of the hypermoderns can be carried to extremes. Nowadays, both views are seen as correct. A distillation of the two philosophies is needed to cope successfully with any particular situation. *See also* Classical.

Initiative: When you are able to make threats to which your opponent must react, you are said to *possess the initiative*.

Innovation: A new move in an established opening.

Intuition: Finding the right move or strategy by "feel" rather than by calculation.

Isolated Pawn: A pawn with no like-colored pawns on either adjacent file. The drawbacks of an isolated pawn are that it is not guarded by a friendly pawn and that the square directly in front of it can make a nice home for an enemy piece, because no pawns can chase that piece away. On the other hand, an isolated pawn has plenty of space and controls squares on the open (or half-open) files on either side of it, with the result that minor pieces and Rooks of the same color usually become active. An isolated pawn is, however, considered a weakness.

Kingside: The half of the board made up of the e, f, g, and h files. Kingside pieces are the King, the Bishop next to it, the Knight next to the Bishop, and the Rook next to the Knight. *See also* Queenside.

Liquidation: A series of trades culminating in a drawn or won endgame. Defensively, liquidation is used to trade attacking pieces and neutralize the force of an enemy assault.

Luft: A German term that means *air*. By extension, it means *to give the King breathing room*. It describes a pawn move made in front of the King of the same color to avoid Back Rank Mate possibilities.

Major Pieces: Queens and Rooks. Also called *heavy pieces*.

Maneuver: A series of seemingly nonaggressive moves designed to favorably redeploy the pieces. A maneuver is carried out with a strategic goal in mind.

Master: In the U.S., a player with a rating of 2200 or more. If a player's rating drops below 2200, the title is rescinded. *See also* Grandmaster.

Mate: Short for *checkmate*.

Material: All the pieces and pawns. A *material advantage* is when a player has more pieces on the board than his opponent or has pieces of greater value. *See also* Point Count.

Mating Attack: An attack on the enemy King, with checkmate as the ultimate goal.

Middlegame: The phase between the opening and the endgame.

Minor Pieces: The Bishops and Knights.

Mobility: Freedom of movement for the pieces.

Notation: *See* Algebraic Notation.

Occupation: A Rook or Queen that controls a file or rank is said to *occupy* that file or rank. A piece is said to occupy the square it is sitting on.

Open: Short for *open game* or *open file*. Also refers to a type of tournament in which any strength of player can participate. Though a player often ends up with opponents who are stronger or weaker than himself, the prizes are usually structured around different rating groups, with prizes for the top scorers in each group. Such open tournaments are extremely popular in the United States. *See also* Open File; Open Game.

Open File: A vertical column of eight squares that is free of pawns. Rooks reach their maximum potential when placed on open files or open ranks.

Open Game: A position characterized by many open ranks, files, or diagonals and few center pawns. A lead in development becomes very important in positions of this type.

Opening: The start of a game, incorporating the first dozen or so moves. The basic goals of an opening are to

- Develop pieces as quickly as possible.

- Control as much of the center as possible.

- Castle early and get the King to safety, while at the same time bringing the Rooks toward the center and placing them on potentially open files.

Openings: Established sequences of moves that lead to the goals outlined under Opening. These sequences of moves are often named after the player who invented them or after the place where they were first played. Some openings, such as the *Ruy López* and the *Sicilian*, have been analyzed to great lengths in chess literature.

Opposite-Colored Bishops: Also *Bishops of opposite color*. When players have one Bishop each and the Bishops are on different-colored squares. Opposite-colored Bishops can never come into direct contact.

Overextension: When space is gained too fast. By rushing his pawns forward and trying to control a lot of territory, a player can leave weaknesses in his camp, or can weaken the advanced pawns themselves. He is then said to have *overextended* his position.

Passed Pawn: A pawn whose advance to the 8th rank cannot be prevented by any enemy pawn. *See also* Promotion; Underpromotion.

Passive: In relation to a move, denotes a move that does nothing to fight for the initiative. In relation to a position, denotes a position that is devoid of counterplay or active possibilities.

Pawn Center: Pawns that are inside the rectangle bounded by squares c3, f3, f6, and c6.

Pawn Chain: A diagonal line of same-colored pawns.

Pawn Island: Two pawns are members of different islands if neither can protect the other. Pawn islands are separated by open files. Pawns that are both doubled and isolated constitute two pawn islands. Having fewer pawn islands than the opponent is advantageous. *See also* Hanging Pawns.

Pawn Structure: Also referred to as the *pawn skeleton*. All aspects of the pawn setup, including pawn chains, doubled pawns, isolated pawns, backward pawns, and so on.

Perpetual Check: A draw caused by one side giving check with each move, eventually resulting in a three-time repetition of position. *See also* Three-Time Repetition of Position.

Pig: Slang for *Rook*. *Pigs on the 7th* is a common term for Rooks doubled on the 7th rank.

Plan: A short- or long-range goal on which a player bases his moves.

Point: A square. Also, in tournament play, the winner of the game earns a point. In the case of a draw, each player earns a half-point. *See also* Support Point.

Point Count: A system that gives the pieces the following numeric values: King—priceless; Queen—9 points; Rook—5 points; Bishop—3 points; Knight—3 points; and pawn—1 point.

Poisoned Pawn: A pawn whose capture is a precursor to a strong attack.

Positional: A move or style of play that is based on long-range considerations. The slow buildup of small advantages is said to be positional.

Postmortem: A Latin term that means *after death*. After a hard session of tournament chess, the players usually go to a special room where they can analyze their game, or hold a postmortem.

Premature: Taking action without sufficient preparation.

Prepared Variation: In professional chess, it is common practice to analyze book openings in the hope of finding a new move or plan. When a player makes such a discovery, he will often save this prepared variation for use against a special opponent.

Problem Child: Slang for a Bishop that is shut in by its own pawns. Such a piece is usually inactive. For example, after 1.e4 e6 2.d4 d5 3.e5 c5, Black should have a reasonable game. However, Black's one problem will be the Bishop on c8, which is blocked by the e6 pawn. This Bishop is a problem child.

Promotion: Also called *queening*. When a pawn reaches the 8th rank, the pawn can be promoted to a Bishop, Knight, Rook, or (most commonly) Queen of the same color. *See also* Underpromotion.

Protected Passed Pawn: A passed pawn that is under the protection of another pawn. *See also* Passed Pawn.

Queenside: The half of the board that includes the d-, c-, b-, and a—files. The Queenside pieces are the Queen, the Bishop next to it, the Knight next to the Bishop, and the Rook next to the Knight. *See also* Kingside.

Quiet Move: An unassuming move that is not a capture, a check, or a direct threat. A quiet move often occurs at the end of a maneuver or combination that drives the point home.

Rank: A horizontal row of eight squares. Designated in algebraic notation as the 1 (1st) rank, the 2 (2nd) rank, and so on.

Rating: A number that measures a player's relative strength. The higher the number, the stronger the player. *See also* Elo Rating.

Refutation: A move that demonstrates the flaw in another move or plan.

Resign: When a player realizes that he is going to lose and graciously gives up the game without waiting for a checkmate. When resigning, a player can simply say, "I resign," or he can tip his King over in a gesture of helplessness. When you first start playing chess, I recommend that you never resign. Always play until the end.

Risk: A move or plan that plays for an advantage while incubating the seeds of danger.

Romantic: The Romantic (or Macho) era of chess from the early to mid 1800s, when sacrifice and attack were considered the only manly ways to play. If a sacrifice was offered, it was considered a disgraceful show of cowardice to refuse the capture. Today, a player who has a proclivity for bold attacks and sacrifices, often throwing caution to the wind, is called *a romantic*.

Sacrifice: The voluntary offer of material for compensation in space, time, pawn structure, or even force. (A sacrifice can lead to a force advantage in a particular part of the board.) Unlike a combination, a sacrifice is not always a calculable commodity and often entails an element of uncertainty.

Sharp: An aggressive move or position. In relation to a player, denotes someone who enjoys dynamic, attacking chess.

Shot: A strong but unexpected move.

Simplify: To trade pieces to quiet down the position, to eliminate the opponent's attacking potential, or to clarify the situation.

Smothered Mate: When a King is completely surrounded by its own pieces (or is at the edge of the board) and receives an unanswerable check from the enemy, he is said to be a victim of Smothered Mate.

Sound: A correct move or plan. In relation to a position, denotes one that is safe from all attack.

Space: The territory controlled by each player.

Space Count: A numerical system used to determine who controls more space. Each square on the opponent's side of the board that is attacked by a player's piece or pawn adds 1 to the space count.

Speculative: Made without calculating the consequences to the extent normally required. Sometimes full calculation is not possible, so a player must rely on intuition, from which a speculative plan might arise.

Stalemate: A position in which the player whose turn it is to move has no legal move and is not in check. Stalemate ends the game as a draw, or tie game.

Static: Refers to an object not in motion, one that is not an immediate threat but that will be around to influence the play for a long time. Examples of static factors are space, control of squares, poorly situated pieces, and various features of the pawn structure.

Strategy: The reasoning behind a move, plan, or idea.

Style: Players approach chess in different ways as a result of their personalities and preferences. The types of move a player chooses are usually indicative of the player as a person. Typically, in a game between players of opposing styles (for example, an attacker versus a quiet positional player), the winner will be the one who successfully imposes his style on the other.

Support Point: A square that acts as a home for a piece (usually a Knight). A square can be considered a support point only if it cannot be attacked by an enemy pawn, or if the enemy pawn's advance would severely weaken the enemy position.

Swindle: A trap that holds or wins an inferior position.

Symmetry: A situation in which both sides have the same position. Often arises when Black copies White's moves.

Tactics: Situations that are based on the calculation of variations. A position with many traps and combinations is considered to be *tactical* in nature.

Tempo: One move, as a unit of time; the plural is *tempi*. If a piece can reach a useful square in one move but takes two moves to get there, it has *lost a tempo*. For example, after 1.e4 e5 2.d4 exd4 3.Qxd4 Nc6, Black gains a tempo and White loses one, because the White Queen is attacked and White must move his Queen a second time to get it to safety.

Theory: Well-known opening, middlegame, and endgame positions that are documented in books.

Threat: A move or plan that intends to somehow damage the enemy position.

Three-Time Repetition of Position: Occurs when the same position recurs twice, with the same player to move and the same movement possibilities. Either player can claim a draw (a tie game) when this happens. *See also* Perpetual Check.

Time: In this book, in addition to the common use of the word ("Black does not have time to stop all of White's threats"), time is a measure of development. Also refers to *thinking time*, as measured on a chess clock. *See* Time Control. *See also* Tempo.

Time Control: The amount of time in which each player must play a specified number of moves. In international competitions, the typical time control is 40 moves in 2 hours for each player. After each player has made 40 moves, each is given an additional amount of time (usually 1 hour for 20 moves). If a player uses up his time, but has not yet made the mandatory number of moves, he loses the game by forfeit, no matter what the position on the board.

Time Pressure: One of the most exciting moments in a tournament chess game. When one or both players have used up most of their time but still have several moves to make before they reach the mandatory total of 40, they start to make moves with increasing rapidity, sometimes slamming down the pieces in frenzied panic. Terrible blunders are typical in this phase. Some players get into time pressure at almost every game and are known as *time-pressure addicts*.

Transition: The point at which one phase of the game changes into another; for example, the transition from the opening into the middlegame or from the middlegame into the endgame.

Transposition: Reaching an identical opening position by a different order of moves. For example, the French Defense is usually reached by 1.e4 e6 2.d4 d5, but 1.d4 e6 2.e4 d5 *transposes* into the same position.

Trap: A way of surreptitiously luring the opponent into making a mistake.

Unclear: An assessment of a position. Some positions are good for White, others are good for Black, and still others are equal. Unclear means that the analyst is unable or unwilling to state which applies.

Underpromotion: Promotion of a pawn to any piece other than a Queen.

Variation: One line of analysis in any phase of the game. It could be a line of play other than the ones used in the game. The term *variation* is frequently applied to one line of an opening; for example, the Wilkes–Barre Variation (named after the city in Pennsylvania) of the Two Knights' Defense. Variations can become as well-analyzed as their parent openings. Entire books have been written on some well-known variations.

Weakness: Any pawn or square that is readily attackable and therefore hard to defend.

Wild: A complicated position that requires precise analysis, but the analysis is impeded by unexpected moves resulting in unclear positions.

Zugzwang: A German term that means *compulsion to move.* It refers to a situation in which a player would prefer to do nothing because any move leads to a deterioration of his position, but he moves something because it is illegal to pass.

Zwischenzug: A German term that means *in-between move.* A surprising move that, when inserted in an apparently logical sequence (for example, a check that interrupts a series of exchanges), changes the result of that sequence.

Answers to Quizzes and Tests

Quizzes

Chapter One

QUIZ 1: The Xs are on squares a2, d5, and h7.

QUIZ 2: Compare your board with Diagram 8, which shows the pieces and pawns in their correct starting positions.

QUIZ 3: White's Rook cannot capture the Black Rook because the White Queen is in the way. Rooks cannot jump over other pieces. White's Rook can capture the enemy Queen on d7, though this capture would be a trade because Black would then capture White's Queen with ...Rxf5. White's best moves are Queen moves, with Qxd7 being the strongest (because it captures the Black Queen) and Qxg5 being the next strongest (because it captures a Black Rook).

QUIZ 4: No, the Bishops can never take one another, because they are permanently situated on opposite-colored squares. Because of this placement, these pieces are called Bishops of opposite color. Each piece knows the other exists, but for each, the other is like a ghost.

QUIZ 5: The White Knight can capture the Black pawns on f6 and d6, or it can capture the Black Rook on c3. With this particular move, it cannot capture the Black pawn on g4.

QUIZ 6: White's pawn cannot move because it is blocked by the enemy pawn on c5. If an enemy piece or pawn stood on b5 or d5, White's pawn could move by capturing it. As things stand, the pawn is effectively immobilized.

QUIZ 7: White's King can move to f3, e3, d3, f5, and d5, and it can also capture the Black pawn on e5. Note that the King cannot go to f4 or d4, because the pawn controls those squares. It is illegal for the King to walk onto a controlled square and put itself in check.

QUIZ 8: White's King has no way to get out of check. Therefore, it is in checkmate and Black has won the game.

QUIZ 9: Black's Rook on f7 can capture White's pawn on f4 (with ...Rxf4, though the Rook would then be captured with Qxf4). The Black Rook on c3 can capture White's Bishop on d3 (with ...Rxd3, though the Rook would then be captured with Qxd3) or the pawn on c4 (with ...Rxc4, though the Rook would then be captured by Bxc4). Black's Knight on a5 can capture the pawn on c4 (with ...Nxc4). The Black pawn on d5 can capture White's pawn on c4 (with ...dxc4) or the White Queen (with ...dxe4).

QUIZ 10: Playing 1.Qf7 is an awful move because it stalemates Black and thus forces a draw (a tied game). However, White can win by playing 1.Kg2 and marching the White King to g6 or h6. Then Qg7 checkmate would be unstoppable.

QUIZ 11: White cannot capture the f5-pawn. En passant requires the passing pawn's first move to be two squares at once. In this case, Black's pawn was already sitting on f6 (in other words, it had moved before) and moved just one square, instead of the obligatory two. If the pawn was sitting on f7, instead of f6, and moved to f5, then White could capture en passant if he wanted to.

QUIZ 12: White cannot castle in either direction. A Queenside castle is not legal because the a1-Rook has moved and now stands on b1. White cannot castle Kingside because Black's Bishop is attacking square f1 and White cannot move his King through an attacked square. When the Black Bishop moves out of the way (say, to f7), then White can castle Kingside if he wants to.

Chapter Two

QUIZ 13: The White Knight can capture the Black Bishop (with Nxe6), but after ...fxe6, White has succeeded only in making an equal trade. White could also consider taking Black's Knight with Nxf5. However, that move also results in an even trade after ...Bxf5. From this position, White's most attractive move is Nxc2, taking a Rook for a Knight (called *winning the exchange*). Always be on the lookout for ways to trade superior pieces for inferior ones. See the discussion of the point count system in Chapter Two, "The First Principle: Force."

QUIZ 14: Black should play the simple 1...Rfe8, putting his Rook on a useful open file. A bad move is 1...Rfd8?, because after 2.Qxd8+ Rxd8 3.Rxd8+, White would have succeeded in capturing two Rooks for a Queen—a 10 to 9 point-count advantage.

QUIZ 15: Playing 1.Qh5 brings another attacker and thus more force over to the Kingside. Remember, the more pieces you can involve in an attack, the more likely the attack is to succeed.

QUIZ 16: No! With 2.Nc7+, White has placed his Knight in a pin. Black is by no means compelled to capture the Knight. Instead, he should play 2...Kd7. White will be unable to take Black's Rook because doing so places his King in jeopardy. To make matters worse, Black now threatens

White's Knight twice, and White has no way to give it more support. Black will win a piece on his next turn.

QUIZ 17: No! You must expect Black to see it. After 1.Nc4 d5!, Black has stopped the threat, and the Knight must retreat. All White has accomplished is to allow Black to place another pawn firmly in the center, with a gain of time.

QUIZ 18: It is impossible to checkmate with a King and a Bishop versus a lone King. Another man is needed—even a pawn will do. The same can be said about a King and a Knight versus a lone King; checkmate is not possible. Try various move combinations to convince yourself!

Chapter Three

QUIZ 19: White obviously has a big head start with his attack because he has a tremendous proportion of his army already aimed at the Black King's position. With 1.Bd2! Qa4 2.Bc3, White has gained the time to reposition his Bishop, by forcing Black to make a useless Queen move. The threat of 3.Qxh7+ (using the pin on the Knight on f6) forces Black to play 3...h5. White can then crash through with 4.Nxh5! (sacrificing in order to charge Black's King; White does not want to give Black any time to form a counteroffensive) 4...gxh5 5.Qxh5+ Kg8 (the pin by the c3-Bishop prevents the Knight from capturing the Queen) 6.Qh7+!! (also good is 6.Bxf6, followed by a checkmate on h7) 6...Nxh7 7.Bxh7 checkmate.

QUIZ 20: Definitely not! Black is already far behind in development. Though he has advanced a pawn, he must start bringing his pieces out if he wants the pawn to live. Playing 1...Qxa2? would move an already developed piece and give White a few ways of winning. White could rip open the position with 2.e5 and then go after Black's King or go for a material gain with 2.Ra1 Qxb2 3.Ba4+, resulting in a discovered attack on Black's Queen by its white counterpart on e2.

This kind of blunder inspired an old chess story. An old man lies on his deathbed. He gestures for his son to come close so that the old man can whisper an important bit of wisdom in his son's ear. The son, full of expectation, moves to the bed. The man says, "Son, if you are behind in development, don't capture the pawns in front of your opponent's Rooks!"

QUIZ 21: You should ignore the pawn. Instead, try to develop your forces and castle as quickly as possible.

Chapter Four

QUIZ 22: White has a substantial space advantage. Black's c5-pawn controls b4 and d4 (2 points) and his f6-Knight controls e4 and g4 (2 points), for a total of just 4 points. White, on the other hand, is doing much better. His a4-pawn controls b5 (1 point), his c4-pawn controls d5 and b5 (2 points), his d5-pawn attacks c6 and e6 (2 points), his e4-pawn eyes d5 and f5 (2 points), and his f4-pawn controls e5 and g5 (2 points). Both White Knights also attack enemy territory: The c3-Knight controls b5 and d5 (2 points), and the f3-Knight controls e5 and g5 (2 points). The White Queen hits d5 for (1 point). White's total is 14.

QUIZ 23: Placing your pawns on the same color squares as your Bishop is a bad idea, because the pawns block the Bishop and therefore cut down on its potential activity.

QUIZ 24: Moves like 2...d6 leave you unnecessarily cramped. Why do this to yourself? Black can fight for space with 2...d5. After 3.e5, Black continues the fight for territory with 3...c5.

QUIZ 25: Avoid trades. They can only help your opponent.

Chapter Five

QUIZ 26: Playing 2.Nf3 allows Black to push White back with his pawns by 2...e4. Now 3.Ng5 or 3.Nh4 both make the Knight vulnerable to Black's Queen. A move of 3.Nd4 leads to 3...c5 4.Nf5 (or 4.Nb5 d5 followed by 5...a6) 4...d5 (with a discovered attack on the Knight by the c8-Bishop) 5.Ng3 f5. Black then has a huge pawn center, whereas White has only moved his Knight repeatedly.

QUIZ 27: Playing 1...Nh5 attacks the weak f4-pawn with the Bishop and the Knight and also with the Rook on f8. By throwing most of his army into an attack against White's weakness, Black will win the pawn and will obtain a material advantage. Note that Black's doubled pawn on g6 is firmly protected by the h7-pawn and is not weak at all.

QUIZ 28: "Doubled pawns are always weak" is a false statement. Doubled pawns are often weak, but they can also serve some useful functions by defending extra squares that a normal pawn could not.

QUIZ 29: You should attack a pawn chain at its base. The base here is d4. If you can destroy the d4 point, then the advanced pawn on e5 will be deprived of an important defender and very likely will fall. Black's best move is 1...c5!, attacking the base. After 2.dxc5 Nxc5, White guards e5 with one piece while Black attacks it with three. White will inevitably lose the e5-pawn.

QUIZ 30: "Usually you can safely postpone castling for quite a while in open positions" is a false statement. In open positions, it is extremely dangerous not to castle as quickly as possible.

QUIZ 31: Reaching an endgame means that you have traded most of the pieces. With most of the pieces gone, it is important to rush your King into battle as quickly as possible. Remember, the King is a strong piece. Use it when it is safe to do so!

Chapter Seven

QUIZ 32: "You must calculate every possible move and countermove" is a false statement. Calculating everything out is always time-consuming, often impractical, and sometimes impossible!

QUIZ 33: "It is important to find out how strong your opponent is so that you can play accordingly" is a false statement. Don't worry about your opponent's chess skill, good looks, or financial situation. Just play the best game you can, and always play to win!

Tests

Chapter One

TEST 1: White has four ways to get out of check. The first is to capture the offending Bishop with his f3-Knight via 5.Nxh4, though Black would play 5...Qxh4+ and White would still be faced with check. The second is to block with a pawn via 5.g3. The flaw here is that White loses the pawn via 5...fxg3. The other two possibilities are 5.Ke2 and 5.Kf1, by which White simply steps out of the way. However, White then loses the right to castle.

TEST 2: This exercise is a good way of teaching the power of the Queen. Though the Knight will try to run away, it will prove no match for the mighty Queen. White has several ways to capture the Knight, but one simple method is

    1.   Qe7

White threatens to take the beast.

1.	...	Nc6

The only safe square.

2.	Qd6

White once again threatens to eat the horse. Note that the Knight's most central squares—e5, e7, d8, d4, b4 and b8—are all covered by the Queen.

2.	...	Na5

3.	Qd5!

Other moves (such as 3.Qc5) leave the Knight with places to run to. After 3.Qd5!, all the Knight's escape squares are covered and it is caught.

TEST 3: You can crown a new Queen in many ways from this position, and I heartily recommend that you play around with this puzzle for a while to test some of the possibilities. The idea is to learn how pawns react to each other. Here is one possible series of moves:

1.	d4	d5	6.	f3	f5
2.	e3	b6	7.	g4	fxg4
3.	b4	b5	8.	fxg4	g5
4.	a3	a6	9.	h3	h6
5.	c3	c6			

Now White has no more useful moves and is forced to start giving up material, when he would really rather just sit tight and do nothing. (This type of situation is called *zugzwang*.)

10.	e4	dxe4
11.	d5	cxd5

White has now lost all his pawns. White obviously did not play well or this situation would not have arisen. Play through the moves and try to improve White's play!

TEST 4: If it is White's move, he can castle on either side. On the Queenside, his Rook would pass through an attacked square, which is allowed. (The King, however, can't pass through an attacked square.) On the Kingside, White's Rook is attacked, but he can still castle as long as his Rook has not moved.

If it is Black's move, he cannot castle on either side, because the Knight on e6 attacks both squares f8 and d8. The Black King would have to move through an attacked square to castle, which is illegal.

TEST 5: The White Knight can't capture anything. If the Knight moves, White's King would be exposed to attack by the Rook on d8. Because putting your own King in check is illegal, White must leave his Knight on d4. This concept, called a *pin*, is explained in detail in Chapter Two, "The First Principle: Force."

TEST 6: Normally, Black would be happy to get his material back with 1...Nxb4. However, in this case, he has the wonderful possibility of 1...Ne2 checkmate. Remember the old chess saying: "When you see a good move, sit on your hands and look for a better one!"

TEST 7: No! Don't play 1.Qxf7?? because it creates a stalemate. A better move is 1.Qh3+ Nh6 2.Qxh6 checkmate. Taking the opponent's material is usually a great idea, but be careful: Greed has a way of blinding us!

TEST 8: Trading pieces with 1.Rxd7 is a good, safe move. A bad mistake is 1.Nd5??, which simply loses a piece to 1...Rxd5 or 1...Nxd5. When you head for a particular square, be careful that you guard it as many times as the opponent attacks it.

TEST 9: After 1...Rfe8 2.Rxe8 Rxe8, Black would not have accomplished much. Crushing, though, is 1...Rfd8!, which threatens the Queen and intends to destroy the Rook on d1, the only piece guarding White's Knight on c1. After 1...Rfd8, White would like to take on d8 by 2.Qxd8 Rxd8 3.Rxd8, but that series of moves would lose the Knight to 3...Qxc1+. Also bad is 2.Qb3 Rxd1+ 3.Qxd1 Qxc1, which gives Black an extra Knight. Take one last look at the difference between the two moves: 1...Rfe8 places the Rook on an open file but puts no pressure on White, whereas 1...Rfd8! makes an immediate threat. Always try to play aggressively.

Chapter Two

TEST 10: Black must avoid 1...Ne6, because of the pawn fork that results from 2.d5. A better move is 1...Ng6.

TEST 11: This position demonstrates a Bishop pin. With 1.Bf3, White wins a whole Rook, because if the Rook on d5 moves, the Rook on a8 will fall.

TEST 12: Though 1...Rxc5 would normally be a good move because it equalizes the material, White can do even better with 1...Rh1+, because he then wins the a1-Rook . This tactic, called a *skewer*, is like a pin, except that when the more valuable piece in front moves, the less valuable one behind is exposed.

TEST 13: Playing 1.Qxe6+ Qxe6 2.Rxe6 equalizes the material count, but with 1.Qg5+!, White forks Black's King and Rook and picks up the undefended Rook on d8.

TEST 14: Playing 1...Ke5 forks the Rook and Bishop with the King. Because the pieces cannot guard each other, White will be forced to part with one of them.

Chapter Three

TEST 15: Certainly not! White is behind in development and is several moves away from generating any real threats. White does not have time to launch a successful attack. An excellent reply to 1.Qf3 would be 1...d5! 2.exd5 Bxd5 3.Bxd5 Qxd5, when it becomes clear that White was never really in a position to attack.

TEST 16: Such two-piece attacks rarely work. Black can push White back with 3...d5 (blocking the checkmate and attacking the Bishop) 4.Bb3 Nf6 (developing a piece and attacking White's Queen). Thus, while Black gains the center and develops his pieces, White's forces are in retreat.

Chapter Four

TEST 17: White: 12; Black: 5.

TEST 18: By fianchettoing his Bishop with 1.g3 and 2.Bg2, White would succeed in placing it on the open h1-a8 diagonal. This Bishop would then be more active than Black's Bishop.

TEST 19: Yes, 1...Be6 makes sense. When you have less space than your opponent, it is a good policy to exchange pieces in order to give yourself more breathing room. Playing 1...Be6 offers to trade Black's passive d7-Bishop for its active White counterpart on b3. If White declines with 2.Bc2, Black would gain three squares in space count, while White would lose two.

Chapter Five

TEST 20: White uses his space advantage to create a new Queen with a tactical trick involving pawn sacrifices. Here's how:

    1.   **g6!**   **hxg6**

If Black plays 1...fxg6, White plays 2.h6!! gxh6 3.f6, and the pawn on f6 will soon become a Queen.

    2.   **f6!!**

This move threatens to lead to fxg7, so Black is forced to capture the pawn. However, now White's remaining pawn on h5 has nothing standing between it and the queening square!

2.	...	gxf6	4.	h7	f4
3.	h6	f5	5.	h8=Q	

White manages to crown a new Queen.

Notice that if the starting move were Black's, he could stop White's intentions with 1...g6! (a big mistake is 1...h6?? 2.f6! gxf6 3.gxh6, which allows White to promote first), which leads to 2.hxg6 hxg6 or 2.fxg6 fxg6!, leaving White no hope of getting a new Queen.

This example may seem confusing at first. Read through the moves several times and then play them over until the logic of the example is clear. It will give you a good understanding of a pawn's potential.

TEST 21: White's position is better, because Black's passed pawn on d5 is firmly blocked and not going anywhere. Though White's doubled pawns on the b-file are not at all weak because of the support given by the a3-pawn, Black's backward pawn is stuck on an open file and subject to attack. By continuing with 1.Qc2 and 2.Rec1, White could put tremendous pressure on the c6-pawn. Here, piece play is more important than pawn structure.

TEST 22: After 2.Rxe5 Bd6 or 2...Bf6, the White Rook would have to retreat, and the Black Bishop would enjoy his superiority. Though 2.fxe5 is a good move because it gives White a protected passed pawn, even better is 2.dxe5, which does three things:

- White gets a protected passed pawn.

- White's Bishop is unblocked and springs to life on the g1-a7 diagonal.

- White opens up the d-file to the backward d5-pawn, which he can now attack by massing his Rooks and Queen on the d-file.

TEST 23: Though Black is ahead by a pawn, his pawns are tripled and are thus more or less useless. White is winning, because he can calmly advance his King and eat all his opponent's men. An example:

1.	...	Kd5		3.	Kg3
2.	Kg2	Ke4			

Now White threatens to play 4.Kg4 and start eating.

3.	...	Kf5

Also hopeless is 3...Kd3 4.Kg4 Kc3 5.b4 Kc4 6.Kxg5 Kb5 7.Kxg6 Ka4 8.Kxg7, which leaves Black with no pawns. Black can't play 8...Kxa3 because White would respond with 9.b5 and the promotion of the remaining White pawn. The main problem with Black's position is that whereas White's pawns can defend themselves, Black's men are helpless and can be easily mowed down.

4.	a4

Suddenly, this pawn threatens to become a Queen, and Black must hurry back to stop it.

4.	...	Ke5		7.	Kg4	Kb5
5.	a5	Kd5		8.	Kxg5	
6.	b4	Kc6				

The feast begins.

8.	...	Kxb4
9.	a6	

and nothing can stop the White pawn from winning its promotion.

TEST 24: Because the center is locked up with pawns (a typical closed position), White's pieces will have more difficulty in getting through to Black's territory. In closed positions, castling can be delayed for a short while without any ill effect.

Index

Symbols
! (excellent move) 7
!! (brilliant move) 7
!? (interesting move) 7
+ (check) 11
? (poor move) 7
?! (dubious move) 7
?? (gross blunder) 7

A
advantage 183
   in force (*see* material, advantage)
   in space (*see* space, advantage)
   in time (*see* time, advantage)
Alekhine, Alexander 141, 171
Alexandria, Nana 180–81
algebraic notation 7–11, 183, 192
   advantages of 7
   captures 9
   castling 10
   check 11
   definition 8
   distinguishing which piece moved 9
   en passant 11
   examples 32
   mastering 7–11
   moves 11
   names of squares 8
   periods in 11
   promotion 11
   reading 7–11

algebraic notation, *continued*
   symbols 7
   writing 7–11
analysis 184. *See also* post-mortem
Anderssen, Karl 5
annotated games xii, 149–68
annotation 184
attacks 184
   discovered 53
      examples 54, 82, 160, 205–6
   double 49
      definition 96
      examples 84, 157, 166
   mating 192
attitude 171

B
Back Rank Mate 48, 131, 191
backward pawns. *See* pawns, backward
Belloti, Bruno 88
berserker. *See* playing styles, berserker
Bird Opening 55
Bishops
   bad 96
   in closed positions 140
   excommunicated 53
   fianchettoed 188
      definition 96
      examples 96, 125, 158, 211
   good 96

Bishops, *continued*
   history 17
   how to move 18
   and open diagonals 95–99, 158, 211
   in open positions 138
   of opposite color 193, 201
   pair of 18, 184
   as problem children 195
   sphere of influence 18
   strengths and weaknesses 18, 95
   two Jans 67
   value 40
Blitz chess 6, 177
blockades 184
blunders 184
book 185. *See also* memorizing moves
Botvinnik, Mikhail 125, 169–70
brilliancy 185

C
calculation of variations 169. *See also* variations, calculating
Capablanca, José Raúl 90–91, 110, 142
   endgame skill 90
capturing 24
   definition 13
   en passant (*see* en passant)
Caro–Kann Defense 187
Castles. *See* Rooks
castling 205
   algebraic notation 10

castling, *continued*
  in closed positions 213
  definition 29, 31, 89, 150,
       185, 207
  examples 32, 203, 208
  history 14, 30
  importance of 30, 56, 185
  Kingside 30, 185
  in open positions 136, 206
  in the opening 27
  Queenside 30, 185
center 185
Center Counter Defense 76
Cessole, Jacopo Da 30
chauvinism 3
Cheap Check 57
check
  algebraic notation 11
  announcing 23
  Cheap 57
  definition 22
  devastating 55
  discovered 82, 160
  perpetual 194, 199
  responding to 23
checkmate 186
  box method 60, 64
  definition 22
  Smothered Mate 197
  versus stalemate 26
chessboard 4
  color 4
  divisions 12
  improvising 4
  Kingside 12
  Queenside 12
  setting up 12
chess computer 149, 159
chessmen 5
  moving 13
  Staunton design 5

Chiburdanidze, Maya 3
Classical 186
clocks 6, 174
  digital 6
  double 6
  improvising 6
  mechanical 6
closed
  games (*see* positions,
       closed)
  positions (*see* positions,
       closed)
computer chess 149
  Deep Thought 182
  example 159
confidence, lack of 171–72
connected passed pawns.
       See pawns, connected
       passed
Costin, Victor 155
counterplay 186
counting space. *See* space,
       count system
Crakanthorp, Lawrence 137
cramping positions. *See* po-
       sitions, cramped
critical positions 187

D
Dake, Arthur 179
Deep Thought 182
defending 106–7
  in the opening
    Caro–Kann Defense 187
    Center Counter De-
         fense 76
    Dutch Defense 163
    French Defense 187,
         200
    Petroff Defense 151, 159

defending, in the opening,
       continued
    Two Knights Defense
         200
  against a space advan-
       tage 107–12
    example 108
  against weak pawns 125
defenses 187. *See also*
       opening moves
Delmar, Eugene 163
devastating check, playing
       for 55
development 74–80
  and Paul Morphy 81
  definition 74, 187
  examples 76–78
  lack of, examples 156,
       204
  lead in, examples 80, 82,
       150–51, 158, 166
diagonals, open 95
digital clocks 6
discovered
  attacks (*see* attacks, dis-
       covered)
  checks (*see* attacks, dis-
       covered)
discovery. *See* attacks, dis-
       covered
Dlugy, Maxim 178
double
  attacks (*see* attacks, double)
  clocks 6
doubled pawns. *See* pawns,
       doubled
draw
  definition 187
  Grandmaster 189
  stalemate 26, 187
Dutch Defense 163

E

Elo, Arpad 187
Elo rating 187
endgame
  and Capablanca 90
  definition 27, 188
  and King 27, 58, 98, 143, 206
  material advantage in 58
  players skilled in 141–43
  with King and Queen 59
    example 59
  with King and Rook 62, 67
  and pawns 27
  and pawn structure 143–45
English Opening 157
en passant 166
  algebraic notation 11
  definition 28, 187
  examples 28, 32, 202
  history 27
en prise 188
equipment 4–7
  chessboard 4
  chessmen 5
  inexpense of xii
etiquette 23, 32
evolution of chess 1–32
exchanging 188. *See* trading
  example 127
Excommunicated Bishop 53

F

face-off between Kings 63–65
Fédération Internationale des Échecs (FIDE) xii, 3, 188

fianchettoed Bishops. *See* Bishops, fianchettoed
FIDE xii, 3, 188
files 8, 188
  half-open 190
  open 91, 192
Firmian, Nick de 177
Fischer, Bobby 136, 157, 171
flanks 188
Fool's Mate 55
force. *See also* material
  dynamic factor 187
  principle of xii, 39–70, 169
forced moves 83–84, 189
forfeiting. *See* resigning
forks
  definition 49
  examples 49, 68, 94, 101, 127, 157, 161, 210
Frazer, Persifor 154
French Defense 187, 200
  and pawn chains 132

G

gain of time. *See* time, gain of
gambits 78, 80, 189
  definition 78
  examples 56, 79, 137
  King's 150
  Queen's 108
game phases 26
games
  Anderssen–Kolisch 5
  annotated 149–68
  Botvinnik–Tal 169–70
  Capablanca–Treybal 91

games, *continued*
  Computer–N.N. 159–63
  Frazer–Taubenhaus 154–55
  Kaprinay–Hubner 157–59
  Kraus–Costin 155–57
  Morphy–Paulsen 5
  N.N.–Goetz 149–51
  playing over 95, 149
  Seirawan–Belloti 88
  Taylor–N.N. 151–53
  Teed–Delmar 163–65
  Zeissl–Walthoffen 165–68
Gligoric, Svetozar 171
GM 189
Goetz, Alphonse 149
Grandmaster (GM) 189
  Female (FGM) 189
  classes 3
  draw 189
Great Swindler (Frank James Marshall) 43
gardez 32

H

half-open files 190
hanging 190
hanging pawns. *See* pawns, hanging
heavy pieces 191. *See also* major pieces
Hubner, Hans 157
Hypermodern 190

I–J

initiative 186, 190
innovation 190

international chess federation. *See* FIDE
International Master (IM)
189
isolated pawns. *See* pawns,
isolated
Janowski, David 66–67

K
Kaprinay 157
Karpov, Anatoly 179
Kasparov, Garry 3, 157
Kenny, W.S. xi
Keres, Paul 142
King
in endgame 27, 58, 98,
143, 206
in face-off 63–65
history 14
how to move 14
moving early 153
protecting 23, 56
by castling 30
sphere of influence 14
starting position 12
trapping 55
value 40
weakening 163
examples 83, 150–51
King's Gambit 150
Kingside, definition 12, 191
Knights
in closed positions 140
history 19
how to move 19
notation name 9
in open positions 139
sphere of influence 19
strengths and weak-
nesses 99–103
value 40

Kolisch, Ignác 5
Kraus, Otto 155

L
lack of confidence 171–72
lack of development. *See*
development, lack of
Lasker, Emanuel 107, 142
Last Exit on Brooklyn coffee house 135
lead in development. *See*
development, lead in
Legall's Mate 52
liquidation 191
López, Ruy 27, 30
losing, ways of 22
loss of tempo. *See* time,
loss of
Lucena, Luis Ramírez 30
luft 191

M
Maddox, Jonathan 137
major pieces 5, 99, 191
male chauvinism 3
maneuvers 191
Maric, Alisa 177, 179
Marshall, Frank James 43,
67
Master 191
mate 191. *See also* checkmate
material 192
advantage 39, 43–45, 189
in the endgame 58–65
examples 166, 206
how to gain 43
definition 14, 189
gain of 14, 39
imbalances, example 40

material, *continued*
point count system
definition 40–41, 194
examples 40, 48, 100,
151, 160, 203
mating attacks 192
mechanical clocks 6
memorizing moves 103.
See also book
middlegame 192
definition 27
how to play 115
Miles, Tony 182
minor pieces 5, 99, 192
mobility 91, 192
Morphy, Paul 5, 81, 116
motives for playing chess 2
moves
algebraic notation 11
forced 83–84, 189
memorizing 103
passive 193
quiet 195
reading 7–11
sharp 196
sound 197
speculative 197
writing 7–11
moving pieces and pawns
13–21

N
names of squares 8
example 9
Nimzowitsch, Aaron 130,
184
notation. *See* algebraic notation
numerical values 40–41.
See also material, point
count system

O

occupying squares 192
open
  diagonals and Bishops
    (*see* Bishops, and
    open diagonals)
  files (*see* files, open)
  files and Rooks (*see*
    Rooks, and open
    files)
  games (*see* positions,
    open)
  positions (*see* positions,
    open)
opening 193
  definition 27
opening moves 193
  Bird Opening 55
  Caro–Kann Defense 187
  Center Counter Defense
    76
  Dutch Defense 163
  English Opening 157
  French Defense 187, 200
  gambits 78, 80
    definition 189
    examples 56, 137
  King's Gambit 150
  Petroff Defense 151, 159
  Queen's Gambit 108
  Ruy López Opening 165,
    193
  Scotch Opening 154
  Sicilian Opening 193
  Two Knights Defense
    200
opposite-colored Bishops.
  See Bishops, of oppo-
  site color
origins of chess 1
overextending 193

P

passed pawns. *See* pawns,
  passed
Paulsen, Louis 5
pawn break 185
  centers 194
    examples 206
  chains 132–34, 186
    attacking 132–33, 206
    definition 194
  islands 119, 190
    definition 194
    example 89
  skeleton (*see* pawn struc-
    ture)
  structure 115, 118–19
    in endgame 143–45
    definition 194
    principle of xii, 115–48,
      169
    static factor 197
    versus piece play 212
pawns
  advanced 120
    examples 143
  backward 123
    definition 184
    examples 123, 128, 138,
      156, 212
  capturing en passant 187
  connected passed 186
  doubled
    definition 120, 187
    examples 120–21, 158,
      206, 212
    when to use 121
  in endgame 27
  exchanging 185
  good 129–30
  hanging, definition 190
  history 20

pawns, *continued*
  how they capture 20
  how to move 20
  importance of 115–16
  isolated 123
    definition 191
    examples 123, 126
  in opening 116–18
  passed 129–30
    definition 193
    examples 129, 145, 212
  poisoned 194
  promoting 193
    algebraic notation 11
    definition 21, 195
    examples 129, 208, 211,
      213
  protected passed
    definition 195
    examples 130, 212
  sacrificing 137–38, 211
    example 151
  sphere of influence 21
  stopping 184
  and strategy 119
  strong 129
  tripled 122
    examples 122–23, 213
  underpromoting
    definition 67
    examples 67–68, 151
  value 40
  vulnerable 51
  weak 119–24
    attacking 126, 206
    backward 123
    curing 125–28, 128
    doubled 120
    isolated 123
    tripled 122
    worst enemy of 131

perpetual check. *See*
　　check, perpetual
Peters, Jack 176
Petroff Defense 151, 159
Petrosyan, Tigran 124, 142
Philidor, François-André
　　115
philosophies
　　Classical 186
　　Hypermodern 190
pieces
　　heavy 191
　　major 5, 99, 191
　　minor 5, 99, 192
pigs on 7th 131–32, 194
　　example 130
pins
　　definition 45
　　examples 45–47, 52, 85,
　　　98, 127, 154, 164,
　　　203–4, 209–10
　　using to win material 47
playing styles 198
　　attacking 42
　　berserker 73–74, 81, 107
　　Capablanca, José Raúl
　　　90, 93
　　Keres, Paul 142
　　positional 81, 107, 116,
　　　195
　　romantic 42, 196
　　Steinitz, Wilhelm 107
point count system. *See* ma-
　　terial, point count
　　system
points
　　definition 194
　　support, definition 198
popularity of chess xii, 2
positional chess 116. *See*
　　also playing styles, po-
　　sitional

positions
　　closed 139–41
　　　attacking 140
　　　Bishops versus
　　　　Knights 140
　　　castling in 213
　　　definition 186
　　　examples 140, 143, 213
　　　and Rooks 140
　　cramped 187, 205
　　　example 82
　　critical 187
　　holding 190
　　open 136–39, 192
　　　Bishops versus
　　　　Knights 138
　　　castling in 206
　　　example 136
　　　playing 136
　　open versus closed 141
　　passive 193
　　sharp 196
　　simplifying 197
　　　example 160
　　starting 12
　　three-time repetition of
　　　32
　　wild 200
postal chess 142
postmortem 184, 195. *See*
　　also analysis
prepared variations 195
principles 189
　　advantages of applying
　　　103
　　and you 169–72
　　force xii, 39–70, 169
　　pawn structure xii,
　　　115–48, 169
　　space xii, 87–113, 169
　　time xii, 71–85, 169
problem children 195

promoting pawns. *See*
　　pawns, promoting;
　　pawns, underpromot-
　　ing
protected passed pawns.
　　See pawns, protected
　　passed
protecting
　　King (*see* King, protect-
　　　ing)
　　Queen (*see* Queen, pro-
　　　tecting)

Q

Queen
　　announcing attack on 32
　　history 14
　　how to move 15
　　moving early 76–77, 150,
　　　154
　　protecting 92
　　sphere of influence 15
　　starting position 12
　　value 40
Queen's Gambit 108
queening. *See* pawns, pro-
　　moting
queening square 48, 211.
　　See also pawns, pro-
　　moting
Queenside, definition 12,
　　195

R

Rachels, Stuart 178
ranks 8, 196
rating system 187, 196
reading chess moves. *See*
　　algebraic notation
recapturing material 14

resigning
  examples 78, 155, 157, 159
  how to 25, 196
romantic 196. *See also* playing styles, romantic
Rooks
  announcing attack on 32
  and Castles 16
  doubled 131
  history 16
  how to move 16
  and open files 91–95, 100,
    121, 133, 140, 158
    examples 83, 89, 130
  on 7th 130–32
  sphere of influence 16
  strengths and weak-
    nesses 91
  value 40
Root, Alexey Rudolph 178
Rubinstein, Akiba 142
Rudolph Root, Alexey 178
rules
  capturing 13
  castling 29, 31, 89, 150,
    185, 207
  check and checkmate 22
  en passant 28, 187
  losing, ways of 22
  moving pieces and
    pawns 13–21
  promotion (*see* pawns,
    promoting)
  resigning 25
  setting up board 12
  stalemate 25
  three-time repetition of
    position 32
  time limits 6
  touch move 32
  winning, ways of 6
Ruy López Opening 165

S
sacrificing. *See also* gambits
  definition 196
  examples 83, 204
  pawns 138. *See also*
    pawns, sacrificing
Scholar's Mate 52
Scotch Opening 154
Seirawan, Yasser 88,
    134–36, 177–79
setting up board 12
Sicilian Defense 138
simplifying. *See* trading
skewers 210
Smothered Mate 57, 197
Smyslov, Vasily 142
space
  advantage 184
  and Bishops 95–99
  definition 87
  examples 166
  how to use 91–103
  and Knights 99–103
  in opening 104–5
  and Rooks 91–95
  count system
    definition 87–89, 197
    examples 88, 91–92, 95,
      100, 110, 112, 117,
      205, 211
    and Knights 99
    and pawns 104
  definition 197
  disadvantage 93
  principle of xii, 87–113, 169
square, queening 48, 211.
    See also pawns, pro-
    moting
squares. *See also* space
  names of 8
squeezing your opponent 87

stalemate
  avoiding 62
  definition 25–26, 197
  examples 26, 67, 202, 209
  history 26
  versus checkmate 26
static 197
Staunton, Howard 5
Steinitz, Wilhelm 6, 106–7,
    116
strategy 197
stress 171
style. *See* playing styles
support points 198
symmetry 198

T
tactics
  definition 198
  forks. *See* forks
  pins. *See* pins
Tal, Mikhail 141, 169–70
Tartakower, Saviely 115
Taubenhaus, Jean 154
Taylor, John Odin Howard
    151
teamwork, example 84
Teed, Frank Melville 163
tempi. *See* time
tempo. *See* time
territory. *See also* space
  Black's 87
  personal 87
  White's 87
threats 198
three-time repetition of po-
    sition 199
  definition 32
tied game. *See* draw
time. *See also* clocks
  advantage 71–73

time, *continued*
  definition 71
  and development. *See*
    development
  examples 72–73
  how to use 82–85
  controls 199
  definition 199
  dynamic factor 187
  gain of 77, 117
    examples 152, 156
  limits 6, 199
  loss of 75–76, 198
    examples 75–76, 152,
      154
  pressure 199
  principle of xii, 71–86,
    169
  violating 105
timers 5–7, 174
touch move, rule 32
trading 188, 205
  to defend against a space
    advantage 110
  examples 155, 203
  to gain space 211
    examples 160
transition 199
transposing 200
traps 24, 48, 200
  Cheap Check 57
  Excommunicated Bishop
    53
  Fool's Mate 55

traps, *continued*
  and King 55–58
  laying 50
  Legall's Mate 52
  Scholar's Mate 52
  and undefended pieces
    53–55
  and weak pawns 51–53
Treybal, Karel 91
tripled pawns. *See* pawns,
  tripled
two Jans 67
Two Knights Defense
  200

U–V
underpromoting pawns.
  See pawns, under-
  promoting
U.S. Championship 176
values. *See also* material,
  point count system
  assigning to chessmen
    40–41
variations
  calculating 45, 169, 185,
    207
  definition 200
  prepared 195

W
Walthoffen, Walter Von 165

weak pawns. *See* pawns,
  weak
weaknesses 200
WGM 3, 189
WIM 3
winning 22
  by squeezing your oppo-
    nent 87
  ways of 6
Woman Grandmaster
  (WGM) 3, 189
Woman International Mas-
  ter (WIM) 3
women in chess 3
World Champions
  Alekhine, Alexander 171
  Botvinnik, Mikhail 169–70
  first 1
  Karpov, Anatoly 179
  Kasparov, Garry 3, 157
  Petrosyan, Tigran 124
  Steinitz, Wilhelm 106
  Tal, Mikhail 169–70
  women's 3
writing chess moves. *See* al-
  gebraic notation

Z
Zeissl 165
zugzwang 200
  definition 97
  examples 97, 208
zwischenzug 200

Yasser Seirawan

International Grandmaster Yasser Seirawan is considered the top U.S. contender for the chess World Champion title. The only American contender for the world title since Bobby Fischer retired in 1975, Seirawan won the U.S. Champion title for the third time in 1989. That same year, he also won the U.S. Blitz Champion title. In tournament play, he has defeated both Garry Kasparov and Anatoly Karpov, the two top-ranking players in the world. He is the only American to have played in the World Cup cycle. Playing against Kasparov and Karpov, he tied for third place in the final World Cup tournament. He was a member of the '80, '82, '86, and '88 U.S. Olympic teams.

Born in Damascus, Syria, in 1960, Seirawan moved to Seattle at the age of seven. His chess career was launched at the age of twelve, when he began to play in (and win) local and regional tournaments. Seirawan currently lives in Seattle, Washington, where he is the owner and editor of *Inside Chess* magazine.

Jeremy Silman

International Master Jeremy Silman tied for first place in the 1990 National Open tournament. He also tied for first place in the 1982 U.S. Open. He is a former Pacific Northwest Champion and a former Washington State Champion.

Silman has written extensively about chess. He is the author of 16 books, and his magazine articles have been published all over the world. He has produced a video and a computer program. Silman now lives in Beverly Hills, California.

The manuscript for this book was prepared and submitted to Microsoft Press in electronic form. Text files were processed and formatted using Microsoft Word.

Principal word processor: Joan Anderson
Principal proofreader: Polly Fox Urban
Principal typographer: Kjell Swedin
Linotronic technician: Carol L. Luke
Interior text designer: Darcie S. Furlan
Cover color separator: Rainier Color

The chessboard graphics were created with the Arts & Letters Editor from Computer Support Corporation, Dallas, Texas.

Text composition by Online Press Inc. in Century Old Style with display type in Optima Bold, using Ventura Publisher and the Linotronic 300 laser imagesetter.

Printed on recycled paper stock.

SILVER FALLS LIBRARY
410 South Water St.
Silverton, OR 97381
(503) 873-5173